WARPLANES
of the 20TH CENTURY

Christopher Chant

Illustrated by John Batchelor

TIGER BOOKS INTERNATIONAL
LONDON

This edition published in 1996 by
Tiger Books International PLC, Twickenham
© Graham Beehag Books, Christchurch, Dorset
All rights reserved
Printed and bound in Singapore

ISBN 1-85501-807-1

WARPLANES

of the 20TH CENTURY

Contents

6
World War I: The Birth of Military Aviation

32
Sad Years of Retrenchment

46
World War II in the Air

81
The Age of Turbine Propulsion

121
Through the Present and Into the Future

140
Glossary

143
Index

World War I: The Birth of Military Aviation

THE widespread use of aircraft in World War I (1914-18) altered both the nature of aviation and public opinion about flight and fliers. Although aircraft had seen extremely limited use as military weapons in the last few years before World War I, in 1914 most Europeans still considered flight to be the province of adventurous spirits who flew for sport and for excitement, without any real practical purpose. By the end of the conflict aviation was very big business, however, for many thousands of aircraft and engines had been built in a multitude of factories, most of which had no connection with aviation before the start of hostilities in August 1914. The air forces of the combatants, too, had grown into potent weapons of war, revealing to the far-sighted the potential that in World War II (1939-45) was to usher in the era of total war in which every man, woman and child, no matter how remote from the actual fighting front, was liable to attack.

Yet when World War I started few foresaw what was about to happen, for the role of aircraft was still uncertain. Although experiments with armament, principally light machine-guns and small bombs, had been carried out before the war, general military enthusiasm for the concept of armed aircraft had been lukewarm at best. This was understandable to a certain extent, for the already limited performance of most types of aircraft was seriously hampered by the addition of extra weight in the form of armament. Most generals could see little real scope for the employment of aircraft in war, nor could they see any purpose to be served by providing aircraft with armament to shoot at other aircraft serving in a similarly ill-defined role.

Despite military authorities' refusal to study the benefits and disadvantages of aircraft with any insight, enthusiasts called for aircraft to take their place in the nations' armed forces. This pressure, combined with a desire not to allow any one country to take a lead in building an air force, eventually led the French, German, British and other European governments to sanction the introduction of aircraft into their military forces. France and Germany soon led the field, and public indignation about this continental lead then forced the British government to spend more generously on their forces.

Thus the armed forces now had aircraft. But what were they to do with them, and how best were the services to exploit these expensive machines and the equally expensive force of men to fly and maintain them? The only possible solution in the years immediately preceding World War I seemed to be reconnaissance of two types: firstly tactical or strategic reconnaissance

Entering service in 1917 as an evolutionary development of the S.7, the SPAD S.13 was one of the finest fighters of World War I through its combination of excellent performance, adequate agility, considerable strength and great steadiness as a platform for its armament of two 0.303in (7.7mm) Vickers machine-guns installed in the upper part of the forward fuselage and fitted with synchronisation equipment so that they could fire through the disc swept by the propeller without hitting either of its two vital blades. Powered by a 235hp Hispano-Suiza 8Be water-cooled engine, the S.13 had a maximum level speed of 138mph (222km/h) at 6,560ft (2,000m), a ceiling of 21,800ft (6,645m), and an endurance of 2 hours. The fighter spanned 26ft 10.875in (9.84m) and was 20ft 8in (6.30m) long, and its weights included an empty figure of 1,257lb (570kg) and a maximum take-off figure of 1,808lb (820kg). During World War I, the S.13 equipped one Belgian, 81 French, 16 American and 11 Italian squadrons, and after the war was also escorted to Belgium, Czechoslovakia, Japan and Poland.

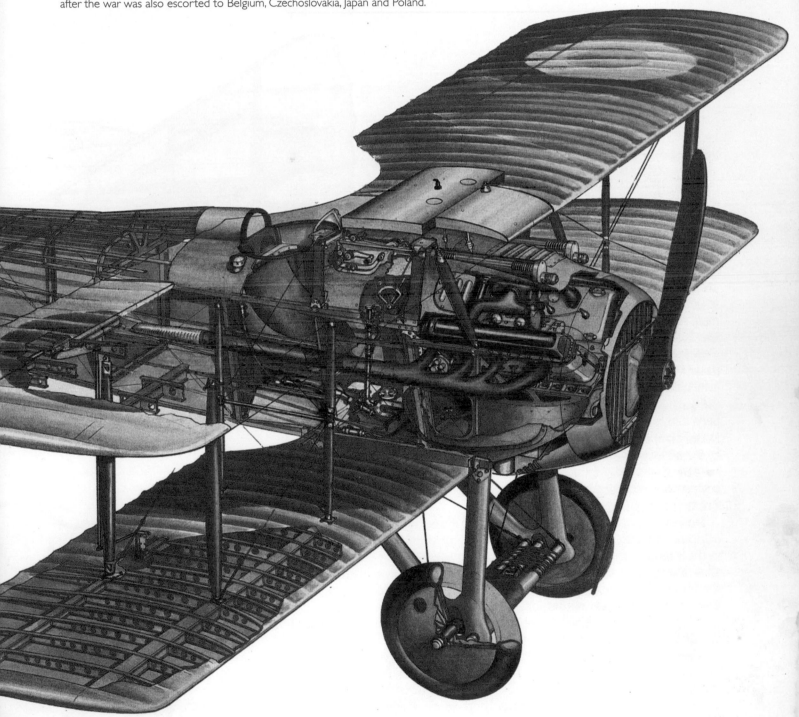

for commanders, and secondly spotting for the artillery. In the former, it was hoped, a trained officer would be able to use the vantage point the aircraft gave him to observe and note down enemy dispositions and movements and then report them to his command. In the latter an officer could spot the fall of his battery's shot, and then issue corrections which could be delivered in a weighted container, by signalling with manoeuvres or, it was hoped, by radio once a suitably light transmitter had been developed. France and Germany, both of whom placed great reliance on artillery, were quick to adopt the role of artillery spotting for their air forces. The United Kingdom, however, still lagged behind technically and theoretically, despite the efforts of many junior officers, and until 1914 its air forces were seen as an unwanted supplement to the cavalry in the latter's traditional capacity as light reconnoitring forces.

The various military aircraft competitions held in 1911 and 1912 had been intended to produce types that could be standardised for the squadrons, thus easing procurement and maintenance problems. Yet it was one thing to select what was considered a type suitable for widespread use, and another to get it into 'mass production' and thus into widespread service. The aviation industry of the period was just not geared to mass production: most factories had experience only in the building of 'one-off' types for designers or for very limited production. The result, in military terms, was that chosen designs could not as yet be built in sufficient quantity and there could be little standardisation of types within the squadrons.

In this respect the Germans and French were better off than the British. The Germans fielded a large number of Taube (dove) types derived from the experiments of Etrich and Wels, as well as units homogeneously equipped with tractor biplanes of Albatros and Aviatik design. The French had squadrons of Voisin bombers, and Blériots and Morane-Saulniers for reconnaissance work.

Above: The B.E.2a was a product of the Royal Aircraft Factory at Farnborough, and was in many ways an excellent aeroplane inasmuch as it was strong, possessed no handling vices, and was inherently stable. Experience in World War I soon showed, however, that while it promoted basic flight safety, inherent stability was a hindrance to effective operational use as it made rapid manoeuvring very difficult.

The British, almost inevitably, went to war with several French aircraft plus a large miscellany of British types, the best of which were the Royal Aircraft Factory's Blériot Experimental (B.E.) 2, the Sopwith Tabloid, the Bristol Scout D and various marks of Avro Type 504.

During the first stages of the war, the Allied powers operated 233 aircraft (160 French and 73 British in France) against the Germans' total of 246. At first the weather was superb, but the aircraft had not been designed for intensive operations and their serviceability was low, a factor compounded by the number of different types and engines in service at a time when the Allies were in full retreat and all logistical backing was run on an extemporised basis. Losses were tolerable, however, and the Royal Flying Corps (RFC) began to turn in useful reconnaissance reports. At first the high command was loath to heed the information received from this novel source, but when British reconnaissance aeroplanes brought in the first news of the Germans' great left wheel to sweep down past the west side of Paris, information which was subsequently confirmed by orthodox methods, the generals at last began to realise that in aircraft they had an important new aid. The art of camouflage against air reconnaissance was as yet unknown, and so the observers of the 'recce-jobs' had an easy time and could turn in useful information.

Although their primary tasks were reconnaissance and artillery spotting when the front was stable, the young and adventurous pilots of the day saw no reason why both sides should enjoy such benefits, when it might be possible to prevent the enemy from acquiring information by simply shooting at him and perhaps forcing him down. It was not long, therefore, before the first weapons made their appearance in the air. Initially these weapons consisted of personal equipment such as rifles and pistols. The resultant aerial duels stood little chance of inflicting mortal damage on the combatants. More hopeful, or perhaps just less realistic, innovators tried shotguns, hand grenades, bricks and even grappling hooks on the end of lengths of cord, the last of which it was hoped would hit and destroy the enemy's propeller. Others decided that flying close to the enemy might cause the pilot's nerve to fail and so cause him to come down. In fact, this last tactic was used against the first aeroplane verifiably forced down in combat, when a German two-seater was brought down by the aerial antics of three pilots from No. 2 Squadron, RFC, led by Lieutenant H. D. Harvey-Kelly on 25 August 1914.

The B classification was used by the Germans in the first part of World War I to signify their unarmed reconnaissance aircraft, and the mainstays of this force in the first part of the war were the Albatros B I and B II, here epitomised by the B II that was in essence a scaled-down version of the B I with the same arrangement of the pilot in the rear seat with the observer in the front seat. Operational experience soon revealed the inadequacy of this arrangement, for the observer had only very limited fields of vision from the front cockpit, and later aircraft reversed this arrangement to locate the observer in the rear cockpit, where he was also provided with a trainable machine-gun for defence of the aeroplane from rearward attack. The B II was powered by a 100hp Mercedes D.I water-cooled engine, and its performance included a maximum speed of 65mph (105km/h) at sea level, a ceiling of 9,845ft (3,000m) and endurance of 4 hours. The type had empty and maximum take-off weights of 1,591 and 2,361lb (722 and 1,070kg) respectively, and its dimensions included a span of 42ft 0in (12.80m) and length of 25ft 0.375in (7.63m).

It was only a matter of time before effective aerial armament began to take effect, and on 5 October a French gunner, one Caporal Quénault, shot down an Aviatik two-seater with a Hotchkiss machine-gun mounted in the front of the nacelle of a Voisin bomber flown by Sergeant Joseph Frantz. From this time onwards the incidence of aerial combats, and also of aerial victories, began slowly to climb. But there remained one basic problem to be solved before air combat could be undertaken on a large scale, and this factor of interference between gun and propeller was not to be solved until 1915.

It had also occurred to various pilots that if one could fly over a target, then one could also drop missiles on it, and early in the war practical work began on the development of bombing. As early as June 1910 the indefatigable Glenn Curtiss had dropped dummy bombs on the outline of a battleship buoyed out on Lake Keuka, New York. Bombing competitions, using bags of flour, had even become a popular feature of pre-war flying meetings. The French and Germans, particularly the former, were concerned with bombing from the beginning of the war. On 14 August 1914, the French sent two Voisins to attack the Zeppelin sheds at Metz-Frascaty, and on 30 August a German Taube dropped five small bombs on Paris, killing one civilian and injuring another two.

The RFC was not at first especially interested in bombing, but its naval sister service, the Royal Naval Air Service (RNAS), showed more enterprise, launching its first, and in the event abortive, raid on the Zeppelin sheds at Düsseldorf with two aircraft from Antwerp on 22 September. Another raid on the same target was launched on 8 October, and this time the Zeppelin Z.IX was destroyed.

Early bombs were extemporised affairs, usually based on an artillery shell with fins attached, and bombing sights were nonexistent. Nevertheless the will was there, and in the autumn of 1914 the French decided to build up a major bombing force of Voisins, which were too slow and ponderous for air combat, but which had reasonable range and load-carrying capacity.

The problem that had hindered the development of true air fighting, that of the location of the machine-gun relative to the propeller, was easily solved on the older, pusher type of two-seaters. A light machine-gun, usually on a simple pillar mounting to allow easy traverse and elevation, was positioned at the front of the nacelle for the observer's use. Even on the newer tractor two-seaters, though the results were not particularly good, the observer could be provided with a light machine-gun capable of upward, rearward and lateral fire. The disadvantage of this system, however, was that the observer

This is the Voisin Type 3, otherwise known as the Voisin Type LA, in which the world's first air-to-air victory was gained on 5 October 1914. Although the aeroplane was a bomber and reconnaissance type, its size and weight-lifting ability made it feasible to install a 0.315in (8mm) Hotchkiss trainable machine-gun in the forward crew position, which was located in the extreme nose as the aeroplane was of the pusher configuration with the engine driving a pusher propeller at the rear of the central nacelle. On this history-making occasion, the Type 3 of Escadrille VB24 was being flown by Sergeant Joseph Frantz with Caporal Quénault as his observer/gunner, and near Reims encountered an Aviatik two-seater of the German air force. Quénault fired 47 rounds, and the Aviatik crashed in flames, killing its crew which comprised Schichting and von Zangen, the former an enlisted man flying the aeroplane and the latter an observer of commissioned rank. It was the German practice of the day to regard the pilot merely as the 'chauffeur' for the more important observer.

(who usually occupied the forward of the two seats so that the removal of his weight, on or near the aeroplane's centre of gravity, would not affect the trim of the machine on solo flights), was located between the wings, which seriously curtailed his field of vision and of fire, surrounded as he was by a mass of rigging and bracing wires, many of which would be cut by bullets. This problem was especially acute on early models of the B.E.2, the standard British two-seater in the first period of the war. The matter was later reconsidered and improved by reversing the positions of pilot and observer so that the observer had an improved field of fire over the aircraft's rear.

Although armament was fitted to two-seaters from the earliest days of the war, two-seaters were not really suited to conversion into fighters, or 'scouts' as such aircraft were then designated, as they were too big, too heavy, clumsy and slow. A single-seater fighter was required, but tractor types were almost universal by 1915 and the problem of the position of the gun relative to the propeller remained unsolved.

If the gun were fixed to fire forwards along the aeroplane's longitudinal axis and pilot's line of sight, some of the bullets fired would almost inevitably hit and damage one or more of the propeller blades. Various alternatives were tried, including the provision of guns angled out from the centreline of the aircraft by about 45 degrees, but the sighting of guns along such great deflection angles was so difficult as to make the expedient virtually useless.

The only practical solution to the sighting problem was to fix the gun along the aeroplane's centreline, so that basically all the pilot had to do was aim his whole machine at the target and press the trigger. What was needed was a method of stopping the occasional bullet from striking the propeller blades. Experiments carried out before the war by Franz Schneider of the German Luft-Verkehrs Gesellschaft (LVG) concern and by Raymond Saulnier of the French Morane-Saulnier company had paved the way, with the invention of primitive interrupter gears which halted the action of the gun when there was a propeller blade in front of the muzzle. But both experimenters' efforts had foundered on the problem of 'hang-fire' rounds. Here the fault lay with the manufacture of the primer and propellant for the ammunition: inconsistencies in the chemical compounds meant that bullets occasionally fired fractionally later than they should, obviating the work of the interrupter and shattering a blade. To preserve these expensive items, Saulnier had fitted experimental propellers with special steel deflectors, wedge-shaped

Early Bombs

THE bombs used by each side in the first part of World War I were small and extremely basic in design and operation. The standard German weapon was the Carbonit bomb, which was a pear-shaped device with a pointed nose, a propeller-activated arming pistol, and a tapered annular stabiliser connected to the body of the bomb by short struts. The Carbonit bomb was available in size ranging from 9.9lb (4.5kg) to 110lb (50kg).

On the other side of the front line, the British used the 20lb (9.1kg) Marten Hale bomb and the Woolwich Arsenal 100lb (45kg) bomb. The former carried 4.5lb (2kg) of Amatol (TNT and ammonium nitrate) explosive and was detonated by an impact fuse activated by a slipstream-driven propeller, but the latter was soon withdrawn from service as a result of its inadequate safety features. Also available to the British was a light incendiary bomb, which was a simple casing filled with 2 Imp gal (9.1 litres) of petrol that was ignited by an impact-fused cartridge.

The British also experimented with the so-called flechette, which was a dart-like weapon some 5in (127mm) long. These were carried in boxes of 500 and released from an altitude of 5,000ft (1,525m) to reach the velocity of a rifle bullet before reaching the ground, but proved generally ineffective even against infantry and cavalry concentrations.

The French bombs were based on the projectiles of their 75, 105 and 152mm (2.95, 4.13 and 5.98in) artillery pieces fitted with rudimentary fins for stabilisation in the air. The 75mm bomb weighed 20lb (9kg) and was a moderately effective anti-personnel weapon, the 105mm bomb was a more capable device weighing some 30lb (13.6kg), and the 152mm bomb was an altogether more devastating weapon weighing some 110lb (50kg).

French armourers bomb-up a flight of Breguet Bre.14 warplanes. Introduced in 1917, the Bre.14 was one of the finest warplanes of French design to emerge in World War I, and was a rugged, high-performance type that could function in the two-seat light bomber and two-seat tactical reconnaissance and army co-operation roles.

items bolted to the back of the propeller blades to deflect any bullet that was heading for a blade. The advent of war curtailed these experiments in favour of immediate production.

Early in 1915 the idea was resurrected by Saulnier and the great pre-war stunt pilot Roland Garros, now serving with the French Aviation Militaire. Probably at the instigation of the headstrong Garros, the two men decided that the actual interrupter gear should be omitted for the sake of lightness and simplicity, the few bullets that would hit a blade being warded off by the deflectors. Preliminary tests proved successful, and in March 1915 Garros returned to his unit with his modified Morane-Saulnier Type L parasol-wing scout. All was ready on 1 April 1915 and Garros set off in search of prey. He soon encountered four German Albatros two-seaters, which displayed no signs of fear or evasive action as the French scout closed in head-on, conventionally a safe angle of attack. A stream of bullets flew out from the nose of the Type L and an Albatros plummeted to the ground, its pilot dead at the controls. Before the astounded Germans could react, Garros had turned and fired at another Albatros, which immediately burst into flames and crashed. The remaining two Albatroses fled, taking with them the first news of the arrival of the 'era of the true fighter aeroplane'.

German pilots consequently avoided any Type L encountered, but in the next 17 days Garros managed to hit another three aircraft, thus becoming the world's first 'ace' fighter pilot. Although the Germans were mystified by this French success, the secret was soon to fall into their hands: on 19 April, Garros was forced down behind the German lines as the result of an inevitable engine failure. In the course of almost three weeks of combat, the propeller blades of his aeroplane had been shaken many times as the deflectors forced away bullets, the consequent vibration being transmitted via the crankshaft to the already highly stressed 80hp (59.6kW) rotary engine. Some form of engine failure had to happen, and Garros was unlucky that the prevailing westerly wind gave him no chance of gliding back over the lines. He was captured before he could set fire to his aeroplane, and was taken to a prisoner of war camp.

Seen here in the form of the aeroplane flown by Leutnant Werner Voss of Jagdstaffel 5 during the spring of 1917, the Albatros D III was the primary reason for the German tide of aerial success known to the British as 'Bloody April' 1917. Nicknamed by the British as the 'Vee-strutter' because of the configuration of the interplane struts connecting the larger upper and considerably smaller lower wings, the D III was an aerodynamically clean fighter with what, for the period was the heavy armament of two 7.92mm (0.312in) LMG08/15 machine-guns in the upper part of the forward fuselage and firing through the disc swept by the propeller blades with the aid of synchronisation equipment. The fuselage was a sturdy semi-monocoque structure of plywood construction, but the wing cellule had one major weakness in the tendency of its lower wing to twist and break away during high-velocity dives. The D III was powered by a 160hp Mercedes D.IIIa water-cooled engine for performance that included a maximum speed of 109mph (175km/h) at sea level, ceiling of 18,050ft (5,500m) and endurance of 2 hours. The D III had empty and maximum take-off weights of 1,454 and 1,953lb (660 and 885kg) respectively, and its dimensions included a span of 29ft 8.33in (9.05m) and length of 24ft 0.625in (9.16m). Voss was the fourth-ranking German ace of World War I, achieving 48 aerial victories before his death in September 1917.

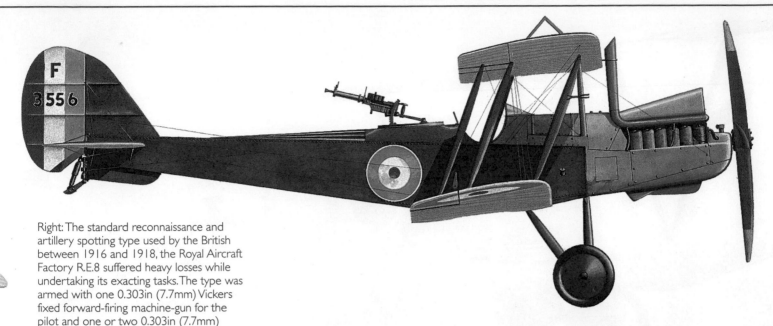

Right: The standard reconnaissance and artillery spotting type used by the British between 1916 and 1918, the Royal Aircraft Factory R.E.8 suffered heavy losses while undertaking its exacting tasks. The type was armed with one 0.303in (7.7mm) Vickers fixed forward-firing machine-gun for the pilot and one or two 0.303in (7.7mm) Lewis trainable machine-guns in the rear cockpit for the observer/gunner, and could carry 260lb (118kg) of bombs. Known universally as the 'Harry Tate', the R.E.8 was powered by a 150hp RAF 4a water-cooled engine, and its performance included a maximum level speed of 102mph (164km/h) at 6,500ft (1,980m), ceiling of 13,500ft (6,125m) and endurance of 4 hours 15 minutes.

Below: The Breguet Bre.14 was the 'maid of all work' for the French air force in 1917 and 1918, but operated mainly in the light bomber and reconnaissance/artillery-spotting roles. In its Bre.14B.2 bomber form, the type was armed with one 0.303in (7.7mm) Vickers fixed forward-firing machine-gun for the pilot and two or three 0.303in (7.7mm) Lewis trainable machine-guns in the rear cockpit for the observer/gunner, and could carry 518lb (235kg) of bombs. The Bre.14 was powered by a 300hp Renault water-cooled engine, and its performance included a maximum level speed of 121mph (195km/h) at sea level, ceiling of 19,030ft (5,800m) and endurance of 2 hours 45 minutes.

The capture of this remarkable French aeroplane was a welcome surprise to the Germans, who immediately ordered Anthony Fokker, the enigmatic Dutch designer who was working for them, to copy the system on his recently introduced M 5 Eindecker monoplane. In just 48 hours, Fokker's team of talented designers and engineers produced not a copy of the primitive French system but an efficient interrupter gear for the 7.92mm (0.312in) Parabellum machine-gun then in widespread use as the standard German aerial gun. (Early in 1916, the 7.92mm/0.312in MG 08/15 machine-gun made at Spandau near Berlin superseded the Parabellum as the standard fixed gun, hence the popular Allied misnomer of the gun as the 'Spandau'.) The Fokker interrupter was tested on an M 5k monoplane and proved highly efficient, and the armed version of the M 5k was ordered into production as the E-I.

The new fighter entered service over the Western Front, and soon earned itself a fearsome reputation. Allied aircraft, which were mostly as agile and as fast as the German machine, could not cope with the technological advance of the interrupter-governed machine-gun, and for the first time in aerial

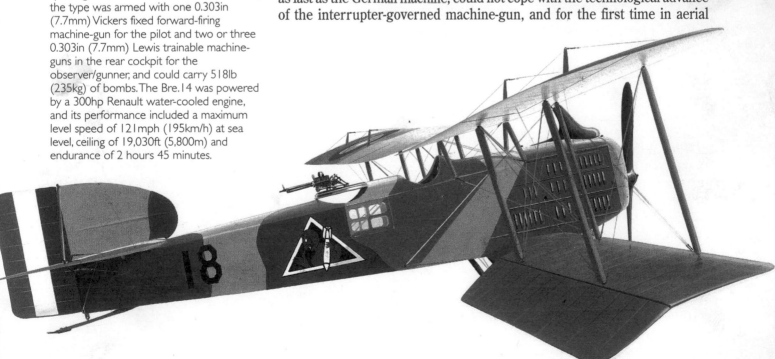

Left: The Airco (de Havilland) D.H.2 was one of the first true fighters to enter British service, an event that took place early in 1916. At this time the British lacked an effective synchronisation system, so the D.H.2 was designed as a pusher-type in which the engine was located at the rear of the central nacelle to drive a pusher propeller turning between the four narrow booms extending from the wing trailing edges to carry the tail unit. This configuration left the nose free for the armament of one 0.303in (7.7mm) Lewis machine gun, which could originally be moved in elevation but was later fixed to fire straight ahead.

Opposite top: These three views highlight the essential configuration of the Fokker E III, which was the definitive version of the world's first true fighter, the E I introduced by Fokker in 1915. The Fokker Eindecker (monoplane) aircraft secured their success solely through their incorporation for the first time in any production aeroplane of a fixed forward-firing machine-gun synchronised to fire through the propeller disc.

Opposite bottom: The Sopwith 1½ Strutter was a remarkable warplane that was built in large numbers and could be operated as a two-seat reconnaissance and fighter aeroplane with the observer/gunner manning a 0.303 in (7.7mm) Lewis trainable machine-gun, or alternatively as a single-seat light bomber with a bomb load of 224lb (102kg) in addition to the pilot's 0.303in (7.7mm) Vickers fixed forward-firing machine gun. The type was powered by a 110hp Le Clerget air-cooled rotary engine, and its performance included a maximum level speed of 106mph (171km/h) at sea level, ceiling of 15,000ft (4,570m) and endurance of 4 hours 30 minutes. The aeroplane had empty and maximum take-off weights of 1,259 and 2,149lb (571 and 975kg) respectively, and its primary dimensions included a span of 33ft 6in (10.21m) and length of 25ft 3in (7.70m).

warfare severe Allied casualties began to accrue. The press was quick to exploit the period as that of the 'Fokker Scourge', in which the prey were 'Fokker fodder'. The emotional controversy that resulted cast the first doubts on the way in which Allied aircraft were designed and procured, especially when no Allied counter to the Fokker was produced.

Over the Front, the 'Fokker Scourge' was at first limited in its effect because the Germans had not evolved a tactical system to make full use of the type's impact. The E-I, soon joined by the slightly larger and more powerful E-II and E-III, was issued to the *Fliegerabteilungen* (flight sections) on the basis of one or two machines to each unit. Luckily for the Germans, prescient officers in the Bavarian air force, one of the several semi-autonomous national forces that made up the Imperial German air service, realised that better results would be gained by grouping the presently scattered fighters into homogeneous units. Thus was born the *Kampfeinsitzerkommando* (single-seater fighter unit), of which three were formed in the late summer of 1915.

The Fokkers ruled supreme in the autumn and winter of 1915, with the Allies apparently loath to copy the German interrupter gear. Instead a variety of expedients were tried, with the result that the inferior German fighters continued to dominate the skies during the crucial early stages of the Battle of Verdun, that military and emotional bastion of France where the Germans had determined to 'bleed France white'.

In the spring of 1916, at last, the Allies began to make headway, albeit still without an interrupter gear. The French produced the delightful Nieuport Type 11 Bébé (baby) sesquiplane, with a Lewis gun firing over the top wing to clear the upper arc of the disc swept by the propeller. The British introduced the Airco (de Havilland) D.H.2, a neat pusher biplane with a Lewis gun mounted at the front of the one-man nacelle. The Bébé first achieved prominence over Verdun with Les Cigognes, an elite French formation that was basically an adaptation and expansion of Boelcke's ideas. The British considered it unwise to group all the best pilots into a few squadrons whilst leaving the majority of the squadrons to cope with mediocre and poor pilots, and instead tended to build up each fighter unit around a few pilots with excellent capabilities in the hope and expectation that their skills would be adopted by the other pilots. This system in fact proved the most satisfactory of all.

After an initial period in which he had allowed his inclinations towards squadrons equipped with homogeneous aircraft to be overruled by his subordinates' desire for a mixture of types, Major-General Sir David Henderson, the RFC's first commander in France, had witnessed the formation of the first homogeneous squadron in July 1915, when a squadron of Vickers F.B.5 'Gunbus' two-seat fighters entered combat. This policy was continued by his successor, Major-General Hugh Trenchard, and the first D.H.2 unit, No. 24 Squadron, arrived in France in February 1916.

The early British objections to homogeneous squadrons had been based on the notion that the RFC's *raison d'etre* encompassed observation, reconnaissance and photographic duties, and so each squadron should be equipped with types suitable for such work. When the overwhelming desirability of fighter aircraft for protection became apparent, most junior commanders were of the opinion that each squadron should have a few fighters that could be sent out with the squadron's two-seaters. The high-intensity offensive operations demanded by Trenchard throughout the 'Fokker Scourge' had killed any lingering beliefs in this system, and the British were now wholehearted supporters of the homogeneous squadron.

Side-by-side, the Type 11s and D.H.2s gradually wrested command of the air from the Germans, taking the air war effectively to the Germans, driving the latters' observation machines virtually from the air. The 'Fokker Scourge' was defeated by April, and the Allies quickly exploited their command of the air by pushing several new types into action in the second half of 1916.

Interrupter gears were now in widespread use on the Allied side, on such types as the French Nieuport Type 17 and SPAD S.7, and the British Sopwith 1½-Strutter and Sopwith Pup. All four aircraft were fitted with a 0.303in (7.7mm) Vickers fixed forward-firing gun, and the 1½-Strutter, so named for

Great Aces of World War I

THE greatest aces of World War I were Manfred Freiherr von Richthofen, René Fonck and Edward 'Mick' Mannock with 80, 75 and 73 confirmed 'kills' respectively.

Von Richthofen first joined a cavalry regiment but later transferred to the flying service and he was at first a poor pilot who never became a truly great flier. This limitation was more than offset by von Richthofen's ability to find and stalk his prey. He was in essence a lone pilot, but possessed the leadership qualities to rise to Staffel (squadron) and then Geschwader (wing) commands, and became immensely popular in Germany for his aerial exploits and skill. Generally associated with the Albatros biplane fighters, von Richthofen finally became an exponent of the diminutive Fokker Dr I triple fighter, which was an extremely agile machine that could be used to good effect by skilled pilots. Von Richthofen was killed in April 1918, probably in air combat with a Canadian pilot, Captain Roy Brown, although it is possible that he was despatched from the ground by an Australian machine-gunner.

Although credited with 75 victories, Fonck was a 'loner' par excellence and often flew without even a wingman, so his victory tally was surely higher than this figure. Somewhat aloof and never very popular with his compatriots, Fonck was an excellent pilot and a truly superb shot, especially in deflection firing. An analytical thinker of considerable ability, Fonck spent much time in the analysis of air combat and its tactics, factoring in every consideration he could imagine, and was therefore well placed in the air to select precisely the ideal way in which to approach his target. So successful was this method that Fonck was often able to down an opponent with as few as five or six rounds: as Fonck said, '...je place mes balles au but comme avec la main' (I put my bullets into the target as if by hand). Fonck survived World War II and died in 1953.

Another whose victory tally is smaller than it should be is Mannock, whose approach to the Germans was marked by an intense hatred and ruthlessness. Unlike Fonck, however, Mannock was a firm believer in the use of several pilots acting together, and for this reason he must be reckoned the finest patrol leader of World War I. Often Mannock set up a 'kill' by crippling the target before entrusting the coup de grâce to a new pilot, who thus learned from the master and started his own victory tally. Mannock was killed in July 1918 after a German infantryman's bullet hit the petrol tank of the Royal Aircraft Factory S.E.5a fighter he was flying.

its single sets of interplane struts and 'half' struts supporting the centre section, also had a Lewis gun for the observer. Much to the annoyance of RFC officialdom, the Pup received its nickname from its scaled-down family likeness to the 1½-Strutter, and despite strenuous efforts to dissuade pilots from using the nickname, 'Pup' was so popular that the authorities were forced to accept it as official. The Pup was in many respects the first adequate fighter. Its performance was excellent, it had a fixed machine-gun with interrupter gear, and its agility was phenomenal.

Unlike many other aircraft, however, the Pup's manoeuvrability was not secured at the expense of other factors, and the type lives in the memory of those who have flown it as one of the most tractable and delightful aircraft ever built. Its control response was smooth, clean and swift, allowing the pilot to place his machine exactly as he wished.

Towards the end of 1916, however, the inexorable see-saw of technological advance over the Front had swung the balance in favour of Germany once again. Realising that the Allies would produce a counter to

The Bristol F.2B was without doubt the finest two-seat fighter of World War I. The type had an inauspicious combat debut as the F.2A with the 190hp Rolls-Royce Falcon water-cooled engine because its pilots regarded the new machine as a typical two-seater and flew it accordingly, with emphasis on defence by the gunner in the rear cockpit, but pilots soon learned to regard the more powerfully engined F.2B as a single-seater with extra capability provided by the gunner. Thereafter the type's success was assured, and the F.2B became a formidable warplane. The type was armed with one 0.303in (7.7mm) Vickers fixed forward-firing machine-gun for the pilot and one or two 0.303in (7.7mm) Lewis trainable machine-guns in the rear cockpit for the observer/gunner. Powered by the 275hp Falcon III engine, the F.2B possessed performance that included a maximum level speed of 125mph (201km/h) at sea level, ceiling of 20,000ft (6,095m) and endurance of 3 hours. The aeroplane had empty and maximum take-off weights of 1,930 and 2,779lb (875 and 1261kg) respectively, and its primary dimensions included a span of 39ft 3in (11.96m) and length of 25ft 10in (7.87m).

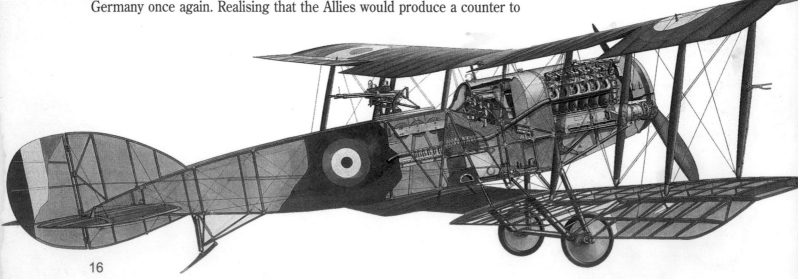

the Eindecker by the middle of 1916, the Germans had set about developing a new generation of aircraft late in 1915. By the last months of 1916 these were beginning to enter service with the Deutsche Luftstreitkräfte or German air force, formed in October 1916 from a variety of flying units. At the heart of this resurgence in German air superiority was the series of Albatros single-seat fighters, starting with the D-I, -II and -III, the last of which entered service early in 1917. These sleek, shark-like biplanes with their plywood fuselages and well-cowled engines were capable of very good performance. Most importantly of all, however, they were armed with two machine-guns, which gave them twice the firepower of Allied types.

The immediate consequence of the arrival of these new German fighters was total command of the air, and, in what became known in the RFC as 'Bloody April', the British suffered losses in aircrews and aircraft of some 30 per cent, their highest losses of the entire war. Most tragic of all, from the long-term point of view, was the loss of many survivors of the previous year's hard times. With these men went most of the practical experience in how to fight an air war, so crucial in helping the new pilots, who were shot down in droves by the 'Albatri' or 'Vee-strutters' as they were known in the slang of the RFC. The life expectancy of RFC subalterns on the Western Front in the 'Bloody April' period was between 11 days and three weeks. Bearing in mind that experienced pilots stood considerably more chance of survival, the life expectancy of new arrivals must have been a matter of hours, or at best, days. A high rate of losses was almost inevitable for the RFC as Trenchard still insisted on offensive patrols and aggressive work even by two-seaters, most of which were by now the newer Armstrong Whitworth F.K.8 and Royal Aircraft Factory R.E.8. Both of these were large biplanes, and the R.E.8 had acquired an unenviable and endeserved reputation as a 'deathtrap'. The fault really lay with the tactical employment of the type, in steady artillery-spotting work, where it was particularly vulnerable to German fighter attack.

Combined with the superiority of the new generation of German fighters, the RFC's offensive tactics served to take 'trade' to the Germans, who were quite content to wait on their own side of the lines. It was the Allies who were attempting to use their strategic initiative at the time, so the German tactics were quite correct. It can be argued that the aggressive British tactics, too, were basically correct despite the enormous losses entailed. Throughout the war, on the other hand, the French kept a much lower profile, and, like the Germans, restricted the amount of offensive work done by fighters. Instead they concentrated on offensive work by reconnaissance, spotter and bomber aircraft, which could more profitably take the war to the Germans. The fighters were used mainly to escort offensive machines, and to prevent incursions by German aircraft into French airspace.

There was also another way in which French tactics resembled those of the Germans. Whereas the British kept squadrons posted along the length of the Front, only reinforcing sectors under real threat or where a major offensive was planned, the French and Germans instead based their air defence on a smaller number of elite units.

On the German side, the *Jagdstaffeln* filled a similar, if smaller, position to that held by Les Cigognes in the first half of 1917. But in June of that year a reorganisation led to the formation of Jagdgeschwader Nr I (1st Fighter Wing). The Jagdgeschwader was made up of four Jastas, as the Jagdstaffeln were usually abbreviated.

Above: Entering service in February 1918, the Ansaldo SVA-5 was a single-seat strategic reconnaissance aeroplane that became one of Italy's best warplanes of World War I. Powered by a 220hp SPA 6A water-cooled engine, the SVA-5 was armed with two 0.303in (7.7mm) Vickers fixed forward-firing synchronised machine-guns, and could attain a maximum speed of 143mph (230km/h) at sea level.

Below: The Hannover CL II was one of Germany's best escort fighters and ground-attack warplanes of the later part of World War I. Intended as a lightweight partner to the C series of armed reconnaissance aircraft, the CL warplanes had a crew of two and a moderately high-powered engine, and in design were optimised for the combat role with compact dimensions, sturdy construction, and good fields of vision and fire for the pilot and observer/gunner. In the Hannover CL II, this last factor resulted in the location of the upper wing at the height of the pilot's eyes, and the adoption of a biplane tail unit to improve the observer/gunner's fields of fire.

By the 'Bloody April' of 1917 air combats had grown into massive affairs involving 100 aircraft or more, a far cry from the individual combats of 1915 and early 1916. The skies over the Western Front were now dominated by huge, swirling dogfights, impossible to follow from the ground except when a crippled machine staggered from the fray out of control, or when an aeroplane which had taken a bullet in the unprotected fuel system plunged down like a fiery comet, trailing flame and black oily smoke until it crashed into the ground and exploded.

The second quarter of 1917 found both sides exhausted by 'Bloody April', the only success of which had been, from the British point of view, the performance by the handful of Sopwith Triplanes, or 'Tripehounds' as they were nicknamed, operated by the RNAS. Although each was armed with only one machine-gun, these were clean aircraft that could combat the 'Albatri' by means of their remarkable rate of climb and their general agility, both functions of the large wing area contained within the small overall dimensions of a triplane layout. So impressed were the Germans that orders for triplane designs were immediately issued. The type ordered into production was the Fokker Dr I, the aeroplane flown by von Richthofen at the time of his death. Very manoeuvrable, the Dr I in fact appeared after the effective epoch of the triplane, and lacked the performance to make it a fighter suitable for any but the most experienced of pilots.

This painting highlights the Royal Aircraft Factory S.E.5a, one of the best British fighters of World War I. The type entered service in the spring of 1917 in its original S.E.5 form with a lower-powered engine, but reached definitive status with the S.E.5a powered by the 200hp Hispano-Suiza 8 water-cooled engine that was later replaced by 220 or 240hp versions of this unit, or most importantly the 200hp Wolseley Viper engine. The S.E.5a was not notable for its agility, which was no more than adequate, but was immensely strong, possessed very good performance, and was remarkably stable as a gun platform. The armament of two 0.303in (7.7mm) machine-guns was typical of the period, but was unusual in its configuration as one fixed forward-firing and synchronised Vickers gun in the forward fuselage, and one Lewis gun on a quadrant over the upper-wing centre section where it could be pulled back and down to rake the underside of any target above the S.E.5a.

Fokker Dr I

THE Fokker Dr I remains one of the best-known fighters of World War I although it was produced only in modest numbers and was at best obsolescent at the time of its introduction. The type was a response to the German enthusiasm for the triplane fighter (after the British had pioneered the type in the Sopwith Triplane in an effort to provide maximum wing area within minimum overall dimensions as a means of boosting agility), and was designed by Reinhold Platz with a welded steel tube fuselage and thick-section cantilever wings that were of fabric-covered wooden construction and fitted with I-type interplane struts only after pilots had expressed concern about the wings' vibration in manoeuvring flight. The Dr I appeared after the end of the 'triplane era', but found success with the more skilled of German pilots who could exploit the type's phenomenal agility in the type of defensive fighting imposed on the Germans from mid-1917. The Dr I was armed with two 0.312in (7.92mm) LMG08/15 fixed forward-firing and synchronised machine-guns in the upper part of the forward fuselage, and was powered by a 110hp Oberursel- or Thulin-built copy of a French air-cooled rotary piston engine, the Le Rhône 9. This gave the Dr I a maximum speed of 103mph (165km/h) at 13,125ft (4,000m), and its other performance figures included a ceiling of 20,000ft (6,095m) and endurance of 1 hour 30 minutes. The Dr I had empty and maximum take-off weights of 893 and 1,290lb (405 and 585kg) respectively, and its primary dimensions included a span of 23ft 7.625in (7.20m) and length of 18ft 11.125in (5.77m).

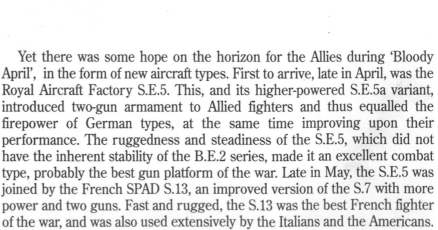

Yet there was some hope on the horizon for the Allies during 'Bloody April', in the form of new aircraft types. First to arrive, late in April, was the Royal Aircraft Factory S.E.5. This, and its higher-powered S.E.5a variant, introduced two-gun armament to Allied fighters and thus equalled the firepower of German types, at the same time improving upon their performance. The ruggedness and steadiness of the S.E.5, which did not have the inherent stability of the B.E.2 series, made it an excellent combat type, probably the best gun platform of the war. Late in May, the S.E.5 was joined by the French SPAD S.13, an improved version of the S.7 with more power and two guns. Fast and rugged, the S.13 was the best French fighter of the war, and was also used extensively by the Italians and the Americans.

Both the S.E.5 and S.13 were fitted with powerful inline engines, but the third new Allied fighter that brought about the eclipse of the German air

force in the middle of 1917 was the ultimate expression of the classic rotary-engined design philosophy. This was the Sopwith Camel, which appeared in July 1917. Bearing a strong resemblance to the Pup, the Camel lacked the earlier type's lightness of appearance, featuring instead a slightly squat, pugnacious belligerence emphasised by the 'hump' over the breeches of the twin Vickers guns that led to the type's nickname, later officially adopted. With the propeller, engine, fuel, oil, guns, ammunition and pilot all accommodated in the front 7ft (2.13m) of the fuselage, where their inertia would least interfere with manoeuvrability, the Camel was supremely agile, especially in right-hand turns, where the torque of the rotary action complemented the turning moment of rudder and ailerons. The Camel's only fault was the result of this compactness and the torque of the rotary action: pilots unused to the new fighter were liable to allow the turn to

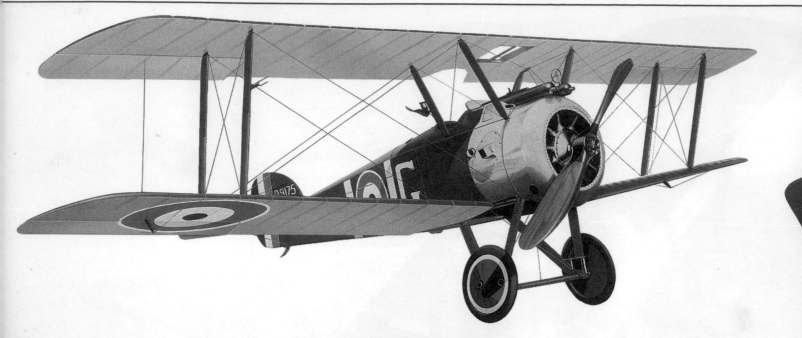

become a spin, which at low altitudes was often a fatal mistake. In the hands of a skilled pilot, however, the Camel was a superlative fighter, and the type accounted for a credited 1,294 enemy aircraft before the end of the war, although later research revealed the real total to be considerably higher.

The fourth fighter to end German dominance of the air, a role it played for the rest of the war, was the Bristol F.2B Fighter which entered service in the summer of 1917. Originally intended as a standard two-seater to supplement the RFC's F.K.8s and R.E.8s, the F.2A version of the aircraft, which had entered service in April 1917, had sustained a rough baptism of fire at the hands of Richthofen's Jagdgeschwader Nr I, four of six F.2As failing to return. But pilots soon realised what a machine they had in the Fighter, with the performance and agility of a single-seater combined with the 'sting in the tail' of the two-seater. Once this lesson had been absorbed and the implications worked out, the Fighter became a formidable weapon.

The Germans were taken slightly unawares by the arrival of these latest Allied aircraft, and were slow to respond. Firstly a new version of the Albatros appeared, the D-V and D-Va, with improved aerodynamics and a more powerful engine, but this machine proved entirely incapable of wresting from the Allies the superiority they enjoyed by the summer of 1917. Urgent requests for improved types were sent out, and in January 1918 the Fokker D-VII was selected for quantity production. This was the war's best fighter, and the acme of the designs of Reinhold Platz, Fokker's chief designer. Originally employed as a welder in the factory, Platz had shown an intuitive flair for structures and aerodynamics, and had been appointed chief designer. Perhaps more important than these other qualifications for the job, Platz was a reticent man who would allow Fokker himself to claim credit for the designs. The hallmarks of Platz's designs were simplicity and strength: welded steel tube fuselages allied to wings of wooden construction but great depth, allowing massive box structures to be used for strength, at a time when other designers preferred very thin sections requiring masses of internal and external bracing by struts and wires. Platz's designs had the elegance of simplicity, and his three most celebrated designs, the Dr I triplane, the D-VII biplane and the D-VIII parasol monoplane which entered service only at the end of the war, were all excellent flying machines. The D-VII, in particular, was feared by Allied pilots, and was the only aeroplane to be singled out by name to be

Without doubt the most successful fighter of World War I in terms of air combat victories, the Sopwith F.I Camel was optimised for the air combat role by the location of all the major masses (engine, fuel, lubricant, armament and pilot) in the forward 7ft (2.13m) of the fuselage around the centre of gravity. This combined with the fighter's low wing loading and compact overall dimensions to produce exceptional agility, and this was further enhanced under certain circumstances by the torque reaction of the air-cooled rotary engine, which made the Camel tricky for novices to fly but allowed more experienced pilots to effect extremely fast turns. The Camel, so nicknamed for the 'hump' covering the breeches of its two 0.303in (7.7mm) Vickers fixed forward-firing and synchronised machine-guns, was powered by any of several types of rotary engine in the power rating up to 150hp, and the most common units were the 130hp Clerget 9 and 150hp Bentley BR.I. With the Clerget engine the Camel had a maximum level speed of 115mph (185km/h) at 6,500ft (1,980m), a ceiling of 19,000ft (5,790m) and an endurance of 2 hours 30 minutes, its empty and maximum take-off weights were 929 and 1,453lb (421 and 659kg) respectively, and its primary dimensions included a span of 28ft 0in (8.53m) and length of 18ft 9in (5.715m).

surrendered in the armistice agreement of 1918. With an excellent BMW engine, the D-VII had outstanding high-altitude qualities, including the ability to hang on its propeller and fire upwards, a position in which Allied types would have stalled and spun.

Luckily for the Allies, the Germans were unable to rush these new types of fighter into service in sufficient numbers to prevent the British, French, American and Belgian fighter forces from exercising almost total command of the air from the spring of 1918, allowing the other elements of the Allied air forces to get on with their work almost unhampered.

The Western Front was not, of course, the only theatre of war to see air operations in World War I. Yet the activities and types of aircraft used over the Western Front set the style for other theatres including the Eastern Front, Italy, the Balkans and the various Middle Eastern areas in which the British and Turks faced each other. On all these fronts, with the possible exception of the Italian one, air operations followed the pattern set over the Western Front, using aircraft 'handed down' after reaching obsolescence in the West. But although the nature of air operations in other theatres followed the lead of the Western Front, each made its own demands on men and machines, principally for geographic reasons. Thus, while such operations may have lacked the intensity of air fighting over France, for those involved they were just as strenuous and dangerous.

On the Eastern Front, for example, the Russians, Germans and Austro-Hungarians had to contend with blazing summers and bitter winters, as well as having to cover vast areas. In the Balkans, airmen had to operate over very inhospitable and mountainous country from primitive airfields, and in climatic conditions similar to those of the Eastern Front. In the Middle East, where yet again it was the Germans who proved to be the Allies' most formidable adversaries, problems of dust, extreme heat and lack of water had to be overcome.

Unglamorous and unglamorized, it was in fact the work of machines other than the fighters which proved to be of primary importance in World War I. Artillery spotters and photo-reconnaissance aircraft shared all the dangers of the fighters, yet received little popular acclaim, the civilians at home preferring to read of the actions of dashing 'scout' pilots. Yet the fighters were there only to protect their own two-seaters and bombers, and to prevent the enemy's machines from acting freely.

Because they had to carry at least two men, armament and their specialised equipment, artillery spotter and reconnaissance aircraft were usually heavy and fairly clumsy. And because they needed to be able to fly

Introduced in the summer of 1917 as one of the new CL class of light two-seaters optimised for the escort and ground-attack roles, the Halberstadt CL II proved very successful and was built in moderately large numbers by Halberstadt and also be Bayerische Flugzeug-Werke. The CL II was armed with one or two 0.312in (7.92mm) LMG08/15 fixed forward-firing and synchronised machine-guns and one or two 0.312in (7.92mm) Parabellum trainable rearward-firing machine-guns on a ring mounting in the rear cockpit, and was powered by a 160hp Mercedes D.III water-cooled engine for a maximum level speed of 103mph (165km/h) at 16,405ft (5,000 m), a ceiling of 16,730ft (5,100m) and an endurance of 3 hours. The type had empty and maximum take-off weights of 1,701 and 2,498lb (772 and 1,133kg) respectively, and its primary dimensional data include a span of 35ft 4in (10.77m) and length of 23ft 11.375in (7.30m). Further development of the same basic airframe with the 185hp BMW water-cooled engine resulted in the CL IIa, but the definitive CL IV with the D.III engine had a somewhat different airframe with the biplane wing cellule re-sited on a shorter fuselage, the raising and lengthening of the horizontal tail surface, and the reshaping of the vertical tail surface.

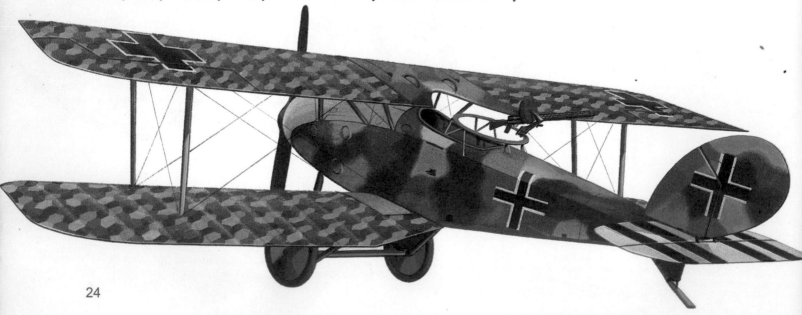

steadily for lengthy periods, a fair measure of inherent stability was called for. This quality had been too much in evidence in the B.E.2 series, but about the right measure was found in the frequently reviled R.E.8. These machines had to operate in all weathers, within reach of anti-aircraft fire and enemy fighters, and so anything which detracted from their manoeuvrability was a hindrance to survival. For all these reasons, the problems of designing a front-line two-seater were formidable, and it is remarkable how many good designs emerged in the second half of the war, usually resulting in the manufacture of aircraft as small as possible to ensure agility, whilst affording the observer a good field of fire for his flexible machine-gun. The Germans produced the Albatros C X and XII, Deutsche Flugzeugwerke (DFW) C IV and V, Halberstadt C V, Luft-Verkehrs Gesellschaft (LVG) C V and VI, and Rumpler C IV and VII. The French had the first-class Salmson 2, powered by an unusual water-cooled, rather than air-cooled, 260hp radial engine. The Italians produced the sleek Ansaldo SVA 10, and the Austro-Hungarians the useful Ufag C I. It is difficult to underestimate the heroic proportions of the work done with these unsung aircraft.

A less important role than that of spotter and reconnaissance machines was played by bomber and ground-attack aircraft, but it was a role which consistently grew in importance as the war progressed. The idea that one could drop a bomb on what could be seen from the air was as old or possibly older than flight itself. The first primitive efforts from aircraft had been made by the Italians in their war against the Turks in Libya during 1911 and 1912. So ineffective were early bombs, especially in the absence of any form of bombsight other than the dropper's eyes, and so small was the load that could be carried by early aircraft that bombing was initially of little use. The successes of a few men in raiding German Zeppelin sheds, however, and the success in terms of propaganda and morale attending the German bombing of Paris at the end of August 1914, made it clear that time and ingenuity would eventually lead to the development of bombing as a useful weapon of war.

Surprisingly, it was the Russians who led the way, despite the fact that the

The Bolshoi seen here was the precursor of the Sikorsky Ilya Muromets that entered Russian service in 1915 as the world's first four-engined bomber. Some 80 of these machines were eventually delivered to the Imperial Russian air service for service in the period up to November 1917, and these machines were completed to a number of differing standards depending largely on the precise nature of the installed powerplant. The Ilya Muromets Type B, for example, had a powerplant of four Salmson (Canton-Unné) water-cooled radial engines in the form of two 200hp and two 135hp units, and its armament comprised 1,124lb (510kg) of bombs and two trainable machine guns for defensive purposes.

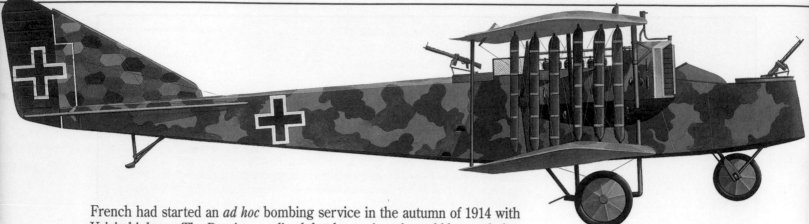

French had started an *ad hoc* bombing service in the autumn of 1914 with Voisin biplanes. The Russians realised that large aircraft would be needed to carry a significant quantity of bombs, and they already had such aircraft in the form of two four-engined machines, the Russkii Vitiaz and the Le Grand, both designed by Igor Sikorsky and built in 1913 by the Russo-Baltic Railway Car Factory in St Petersburg. These were the world's first four-engined aircraft. Early in 1914 the Russian technical bureau ordered 10 examples of an improved and enlarged version, the Ilya Muromets, for the Imperial Russian Air Service. Eventually some 80 of the type were built, but lack of suitable engines seriously hampered operational efforts. Nonetheless, over 400 sorties were flown with bomb loads of about 1,100lb (500kg). In reality, however, bombers of the size of the Ilya Muromets were inefficient even by the standards of the day.

Despite the efforts of the RNAS and the fledgling French bombing force, the Germans beat them to the first serious investigations in the possibilities of bombing. Here they had a head start, as a fair amount of preliminary work had been undertaken before the war during trials involving the use of Zeppelins as bombing craft. First into the field, during the summer of 1915, was the Allgemeine Electrizitäts Gesellschaft (AEG) G II, a large twin-engined biplane capable of delivering a 200kg (441lb) bomb load. This was joined in the autumn by the same company's G III, capable of lifting some 300kg (661lb) of bombs. A year later three other bombers had joined the German air service: the AEG G IV with a 400kg (882lb) bomb load, the Friedrichshafen G II with a 450kg (992lb) bomb load, and the Gotha G III, also with a 450kg (992lb) bomb load.

Though best known as the designer and manufacturer of twin-float seaplanes, Friedrichshafen also produced a number of land-based bombers that were used exclusively over the Western Front. The most important of these bombers was the type illustrated here, the G III with a powerplant of two 260hp Mercedes D.IVa water-cooled engines. This three-man machine could carry a bomb load of 3,307lb (1,500kg) and was fitted with a defensive armament of three 0.312in (7.92mm) Parabellum trainable machine-guns, and its performance included a maximum speed of 88mph (141km/h) at 3,280ft (1,000m), a ceiling of 14,765ft (4,500m) and an endurance of 5 hours. The type had empty and maximum take-off weights of 5,929 and 8,686lb (2,690 and 3,940kg) respectively, and its primary dimensional data included a span of 77ft 11in (23.75m) and length of 42ft 11.875in (13.10m).

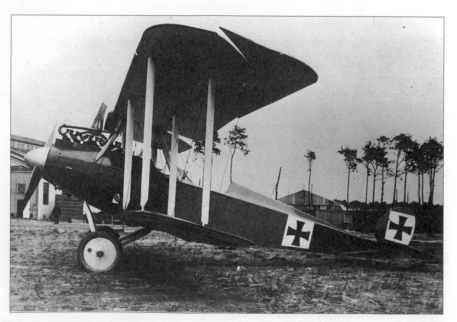

The Rumpler C III two-seat reconnaissance aeroplane was a development of the earlier Rumpler C I with the more powerful Benz Bz.IV engine rated at 220hp and driving a two-blade propeller fitted with a slow-drag spinner, a comma-type rudder with nose-fixed fin, a shorter main landing gear arrangement, a revised wing cellule with pronounced stagger, and aerodynamically balanced ailerons and elevators. The type entered service in the early part of 1917, but all the surviving aircraft were withdrawn in April of that year, suggesting that the type had operational problems, in favour of the somewhat improved Rumpler C IV.

Bombers over Britain

In concert with the Imperial German navy air service's Zeppelin airship raids on targets in England, the Imperial German army air service started a campaign of attacks using land-based bombers. Even operating from bases in Belgium, these lacked the range to penetrate far beyond London, but as the losses of the airship forces began to mount, the importance placed on the bomber offensive increased. Such was the public fear of the raids, moreover, that the British war cabinet appointed one of its members, Lieutenant-General Sir Jan Smuts, to head a committee charged with the investigation of means to combat the 'Gotha menace'. Smuts reported the committee's finding to the cabinet in July 1917, and the single most important finding in the short term was the recommendation that the currently diffuse arrangement of defensive elements should be combined under a single commander. The cabinet approved the recommendation, and Major-General E.B. Ashdown was appointed to head the London Air Defence Area.

Three additional squadrons of modern fighters were soon allocated to the LADA, and in August a 'gun barrier' was established on the corridor overflown by the Gotha bombers as they approached London, and a new system of readiness and patrol routines was created for the defending fighter squadrons, which waited at readiness when a raid was reported as imminent but only took off to patrol a specific area when concrete information about a raid had been made available. The improvements soon made their effect felt, though the squadrons of the Royal Flying Corps patrolling over London had a lean time of it as most of the successes went to the gunners of the Royal Artillery and the Royal Naval Air Service squadrons operating over the coast.

Their increasing loss rate persuaded the Germans to switch from day to night attacks during September 1917, and among the new tactics evolved to meet this different threat was the creation of new 'aprons' of barrage balloons to cover the eastern and northern approaches to London. It was planned that 20 such 'aprons' should be created, each comprising three balloons flying at 7,500ft (2,285m) but later at 9,500ft (2895m) and linked to each other by 1,500ft (457m) wires each carrying twenty 1,000ft (305m) vertical wires, but only 10 of them had been established by the summer of 1918, when the threat of bomber attack virtually disappeared.

At the same time, the anti-aircraft gun defences of the London metropolitan area were divided into geographical squares under the control of a new overall system. The object of this change was that the attacking force would be tracked by sound locators and the information passed to the co-ordination centre, which would then order the concentration of the fire of the appropriate batteries in a 'curtain barrage' over the square through which the bomber force was reckoned to be passing.

The Germans lost 24 bombers to the British defences or crashes into the sea, the latter often as a result of damage inflicted by the fighters during the bombers' approach or later departure, and another 36 were destroyed in landing accidents. This clearly indicates that the perils of nocturnal flight operations were greater than those of the British defences at a time when the interception of bombers by night was still a matter of luck rather than skill.

These aircraft served a useful purpose in paving the way for later types, but were not in themselves very successful. With the arrival of the Gotha G IV early in 1917, however, the Germans had at last found a useful long-range bomber. since May 1915, Zeppelins had been launching sporadic attacks on targets in the southern half of Britain, principally on London, but by 1917 the British defences had been so strengthened, albeit by the removal of squadrons from France, that Zeppelin losses were no longer tolerable. The Germans therefore decided to use the Gotha G IV and V over England, and the first Gotha raids were launched in June 1917 to the total consternation of public and government alike. Although the Zeppelin raids were the first 'strategic bombing' operations ever attempted and had caused a great public shock, the aircraft raids proved a greater threat to life and property. There was an immediate demand for the British government to do something to curb the German daylight raids. The raids continued into 1918, causing a steady stream of casualties and damage.

Only with the deployment of aircraft such as the S.E.5a, which could climb fast enough to intercept the Gothas before they flew out of range, was the threat curtailed. The immediate result of these Germans raids, at first carried out with complete impunity, was the total reorganisation of the British air services. The most important reform was the unification, on 1 April 1918, of the RFC and the RNAS to become the Royal Air Force (RAF), the world's first independent air force.

In 1918, the Gothas were joined by a few Zeppelin (Staaken) R VI bombers, huge machines that could carry 2000kg (4,409lb) of bombs over short ranges. The Germans had a penchant for Riesenflugzeug (giant aircraft), and devoted great effort to the production of a number of types.

The importance, in terms of other factors of the German strategic bombing campaign, far outweighs its military success, which was minimal. The British people, who had imagined themselves immune from war in the personal sense, found themselves embroiled in the 'front line' for the first time. With the realisation that everyone could now be involved in the actual 'fighting', the era of 'total war' may be said to have begun.

Below: Although the D.H.9 had been planned as an improved successor to the classic Airco (de Havilland) D.H.4 day bomber with the two-man crew located closer together for improved tactical communication, the type was let down by its indifferent 230hp Siddeley Puma engine. The promise of the D.H.9 was finally realised in the D.H.9A, illustrated here in post-war form. The D.H.9A was planned as the D.H.9 with the revised powerplant of one 400hp Liberty water-cooled engine and a biplane wing cellule of greater area, though problems with this Liberty meant that many early aircraft were completed with the 375hp Rolls-Royce Eagle water-cooled engine. The result was an altogether more successful warplane offering better performance than the D.H.9 despite a 45 per cent increase in the size of the bomb load.

The only one of the Allies to have devoted some effort to strategic bombing early in the war was Italy, and early designs by Gianni Caproni proved excellent starting points for the Ca 3, 4 and 5 series of three-engined heavy bombers. These entered service in the first months of 1917 with both the Italian and French air services, and in Italian hands they proved to be first-rate long-range aircraft.

The British also decided to use heavy bombers, at first under the impulsion of the Admiralty, whose Air Department head, Commodore

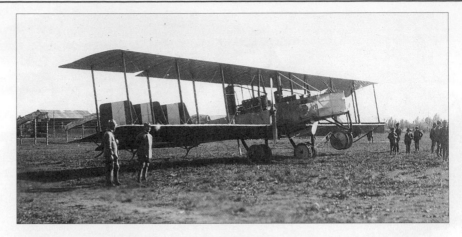

Above left: The Handley Page O/400 was the best British heavy bomber of World War I, and entered service in the late summer of 1918 as an evolutionary development of the O/100, itself designed to meet an Admiralty requirement for a 'bloody paralyser' of a bomber. The O/400 was protected by three 0.303in (7.7mm) Lewis trainable machine-guns and could carry a maximum bomb load of 2,000lb (907kg), and was powered by two 360hp Rolls-Royce Eagle VIII water-cooled engines for a maximum speed of 97.5mph (157km/h) at sea level, a ceiling of 8,500ft (2,590m) and an endurance of 8 hours. The bomber had empty and maximum take-off weights of 8,502 and 13,360lb (3,857 and 6,060kg) respectively, and its primary dimensional data included a span of 100ft 0in (30.48m) and length of 62ft 10.25in (19.16m).

Above right: The Caproni Ca 3 was one of Italy's most important heavy bombers of World War I, and was a four-man machine with a powerplant of three Isotta-Fraschini V.4B engines and an armament that included a defensive element of up to four 0.256in (6.5mm) Revelli trainable machine guns and a bomb load of 992lb (450kg).

Murray Sueter, called for a 'bloody paralyser' of an aeroplane early in 1915. This took the form of the Handley Page O/100, which entered service in September 1916 and proved an immediate success, being capable of carrying some 2,000lb (907kg) of bombs. A more powerful version was designated O/400, and entered service in 1918. This basic type was selected as the standard equipment of the world's first true strategic bomber force, the RAF's Independent Force, and 40 aircraft of the type took part in the largest 'strategic' raid of the war in September 1918, when the Saar area was bombed from bases near Nancy. Only three production models of Britain's first four-engined bomber, the Handley Page V/1500, had been built before the Armistice.

Although 'heavy' bombers pointed the way to the future, their military effect in World War I was minimal, and it was light bombers that played an important part in land operations during the closing stages of the war. Considering their importance, it is surprising that the Allies used only two basic types: the Airco (de Havilland) D.H.4 and its two derivatives, the D.H.9 and D.H.9a, and the French Breguet Bre.14.

The D.H.4 was in every respect one of the most remarkable aircraft of World War I. As well as being very agile and well armed, it had a speed of 143mph (230km/h) at a time when most fighters were capable only of speeds in the region of 130mph (209km/h), and was able to carry a bomb load of 460lb (209kg). The D.H.4 entered service in 1917, and was joined in squadron use during 1918 by the supposedly improved D.H.9, which had the pilot's and observer's cockpits close together to obviate the D.H.4's main tactical failing, the near impossibility of the pilot and observer being able to speak to each other as they were separated by the bomb bay. But reduced engine power meant that performance suffered badly, a factor only partially rectified by the development of the D.H.9a. The French equivalent of these de Havilland bombers was the Breguet 14, which began to enter service in September 1917. Sturdy and fairly fast, this bomber played an important part in harrying the retreating Germans in the second half of 1918, and also proved to be a very adequate reconnaissance aircraft.

While the Allies concentrated on light bombers, the Germans placed more faith in ground-attack machines to support their land forces, as the British had done in the Battle of the Somme in 1916. At first, such machines were modified reconnaissance aircraft used by *Schützstaffeln* (protection squadrons) and *Fliegerabteilungen-Infanterie* (infantry contact units), pending the arrival of more suitable, heavier armoured designs such as the all-metal Junkers J 1, designed by Dr Hugo Junkers, one of the pioneers of metal construction. In the autumn of 1917, however, the need for a lighter type which could fulfil both the ground-attack and reconnaissance roles became evident. This new type was to be operated by *Schlachtstaffeln*

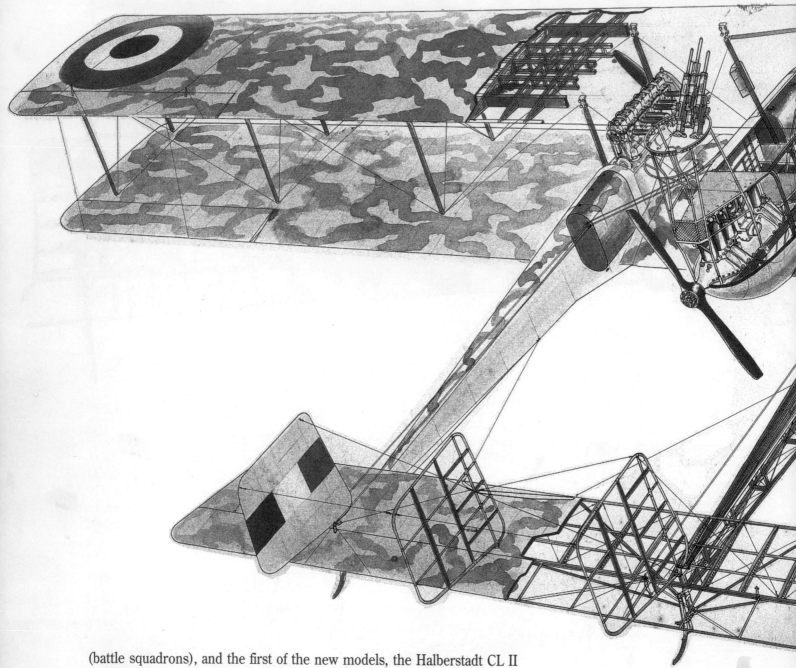

(battle squadrons), and the first of the new models, the Halberstadt CL II and Hannover CL II and III, were ready for the new squadrons to use during the final German offensives in the spring and early summer of 1918. But useful as these new machines were in anticipating one of the major uses of armoured aircraft in World War II, the novel tactics and aircraft deployed by the Germans in 1918 were unable to overcome the clear supremacy of the Allies.

Aircraft had entered World War I as unknown quantities, and their basic roles of reconnaissance and very light bombing were undertaken by aircraft of distinctly limited performance and reliability. Yet, by 1916, aircraft had evolved into durable, efficient fighting machines, capable of exerting some influence on the outcome of the decisive land operations. Two years later, towards the end of the war, aircraft had again advanced in overall performance, and were now to a certain extent the arbiters of the land battle.

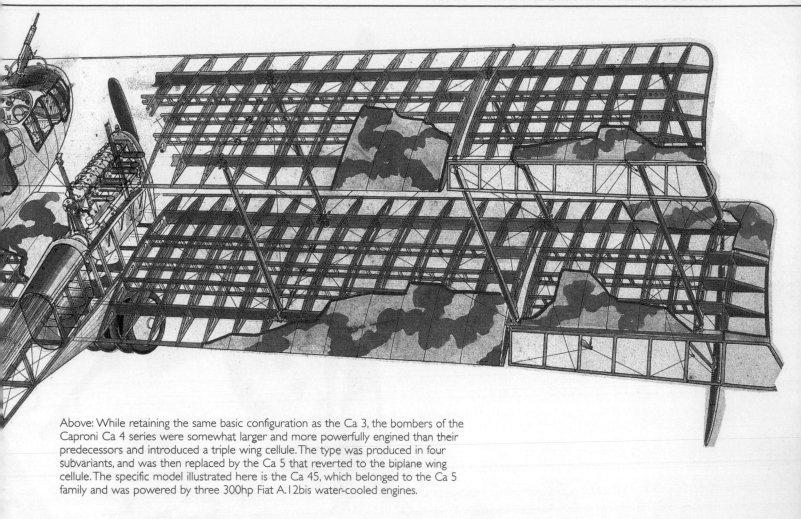

Above: While retaining the same basic configuration as the Ca 3, the bombers of the Caproni Ca 4 series were somewhat larger and more powerfully engined than their predecessors and introduced a triple wing cellule. The type was produced in four subvariants, and was then replaced by the Ca 5 that reverted to the biplane wing cellule. The specific model illustrated here is the Ca 45, which belonged to the Ca 5 family and was powered by three 300hp Fiat A.12bis water-cooled engines.

Below: Under development in the closing stages of World War I, the Farman F.60 was a capable bomber evolved from the F.50 and was the standard warplane of its type in French service during the first part of the 1920s.

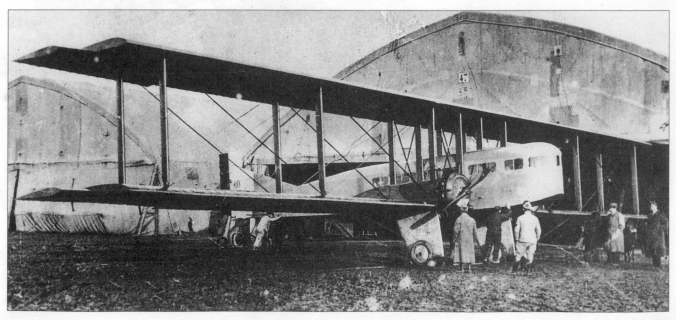

Sad Years of Retrenchment

IF World War I had promoted aviation, the peace that followed almost broke it. For the terrible cost of the war, both emotional and financial, regressed aviation to where it had started in the last few years before 1914, at least from the constructors' and pilots' point of view. In those halcyon days there had been only a few hundred aircraft in the world (of perhaps 150 different types), with about three times that number of pilots. The war had brought vast and rapid growth: by the time of the Armistice in November 1918, France had built 68,000 aircraft, the United Kingdom 55,000, Germany 47,600, Italy 20,000, the United States 15,000 and Austria-Hungary 5,400. The scale of expansion may also be gauged by the number of pilots lost during the war, which was a relatively small proportion of the number actually trained: on the German side, for example, 5,853 had been killed, 7,302 wounded and 2,751 taken prisoner or listed as missing; on the British side 6,166 had been killed, 7,245 wounded and 3,212 taken prisoner or listed as missing.

With the war finally over, it was time to take stock of the consequences. Europe and the United States were dazed by the horrors of the war and the enormity of their losses; the people were all too ready to believe that World War I (or the Great War as it was known) had been the war to end all wars. After years of slaughter it was a natural reaction to turn away from all military machinery, including aviation; and the war's financial cost had an equally devastating impact on industry. Europe was almost bankrupt. France, the United Kingdom and Italy had spent all, or almost all, of their resources on the war and had then gone deep into debt with the United States to pay for the period 1917-18; Germany and Austro-Hungary were exhausted. There was no money in Europe for anything but essentials, and military spending was clearly not essential after the end of 'the war to end all wars'. With the run-down of the world's major air forces, there was no work for the aircraft industries that supplied them.

The drastic nature of the cutback was exemplified by the decline of the RAF in the immediate post-war period. At the time of the Armistice the RAF had 188 operational squadrons, with 291,000 men and women to fly, service and otherwise keep them in the air; by the end of 1919, less than 14 months later, the force had dropped to 12 operational squadrons, with manpower down to 31,500. Although the government soon realised that so small an air

Boeing F4B

ONE of the classic fighters of the period between the two world wars, the Boeing F4B was designed for the US Navy's carrierborne arm and was built in modest numbers for service between 1929 and 1938 as the initial F4B-1, of which 27 were built with provision for a 500lb (227kg) bomb carried on a ventral rack, the F4B-2 of which 46 were built with a through-axle main landing gear unit in place of the F4B-1's divided main units, the F4B-3 of which 21 were built with a semi-monocoque fuselage of light alloy construction, and the F4B-4 of which 92 were built with an uprated engine, a revised vertical tail surface, underwing racks for two 116lb (53kg) bombs, and stowage for an inflatable dinghy in an enlarged headrest. The aeroplane illustrated here is an F4B-4, which had a fixed forward-firing armament of one 0.5in (12.7mm) and one 0.3in (7.62mm) synchronised machine-guns and a powerplant of one 550hp Pratt & Whitney R-1340-16 Wasp air-cooled radial engine. The type's performance included a maximum speed of 188mph (302.5km/h) at 6,000ft (1,830m), a climb to 5,000ft (1,525m) in 2 minutes 42 seconds, a ceiling of 26,900ft (8200m) and a range of 370 miles (595km); its empty and maximum take-off weights were 2,354 and 2,750lb (1,068 and 1,638kg) respectively, and its primary dimensional data included a span of 30ft 0in (9.14m) and length of 20ft 1in (6.12m).

The Armstrong Siskin was one of the most important fighters equipping the Royal Air Force during the 1920s, and is seen here in the form of a Siskin Mk IIIA of which the RAF received 400 for service between March 1927 and late 1932. The type was entirely typical of the thinking of the period, and was a sesquiplane biplane armed with two 0.303in (7.7mm) Vickers fixed forward-firing and synchronised machine-guns and powered by a 450hp Armstrong Siddeley Jaguar IV air-cooled radial piston engine. The type had a maximum speed of 156mph (251km/h) at sea level, a climb to 5,000ft (1,525m) in 3 minutes 30 seconds, a ceiling of 27,000ft (8,230m), empty and maximum take-off weights of 2,061 and 3,012lb (935 and 1,366kg) respectively, and dimensions including a span of 33ft 2in (10.11m) and length of 25ft 4in (7.72m).

force was hardly worth having, expansion was limited to 25 squadrons by March 1920 and to 43 squadrons by October 1924.

More significant for aviation in general was the fact that a new generation of aircraft was just entering service at the time of the Armistice, and it was decided that these aircraft would be sufficient in number for peacetime. Thus the RAF's equipment immediately after the war consisted of the Bristol F.2B Fighter, the Sopwith Snipe, the de Havilland D.H.9a and Vickers Vimy. The first new bomber, the Fairey Fawn, did not enter service until 1923, and the first new fighters, in the forms of the Gloster Grebe and Armstrong Whitworth Siskin, were introduced a year later. Although severe, the British government's aviation cuts were matched throughout most of Europe as well as in the United States.

Aircraft builders found themselves in an extremely difficult position. No new orders could be expected for some time, and production capacity was being run down gradually as existing orders, heavily cut back after the Armistice, were filled. Without military interest, other work had to be found, but this was difficult while the market was glutted with ex-government machines being sold off at very low prices. The majority of aircraft firms went out of business. Those that survived, by forethought and careful planning, faced strict rationalisation. Companies that had bought their wartime premises were now able to sell them, using the capital wisely until business started to improve again in the early 1920s.

For the air forces of the world, survival in the face of political moves to axe military budgets was the most important matter, and the growing belief in the efficacy of bombing as a strategic weapon was a key factor. Invariably, for the bombing theorists, the most important consideration was the weight of bombs that could be dropped on a target. Aircraft speed at first played only a small part in their thinking: there was a firm conviction that 'the bomber will always get through'. British bombers such as the Vickers Virginia, Boulton & Paul Sidestrand and Handley Page Heyford were all slow biplanes, while the American Witteman-Lewis NBL-1 was a triplane.

Only in the early 1930s, therefore, did the need to combine a heavy bomb-carrying capability with high performance gain proper recognition. This led to the appearance of the first real heavy bombers in the United States: the Boeing B-9 and the Martin B-10 were both advanced monoplanes of metal construction, with performance equal or superior to that of contemporary biplane fighters.

Despite the disorganised nature of its air force and aircraft industry, France also adopted the concept of heavy bombing and produced a number of suitable aircraft in the late 1920s. Almost all were notable for their slab-sided, ungainly appearance and singular lack of streamlining. The twin-engined Amiot 143 and Bloch MB.200 bombers, together with the four-engined Farman F.221 bomber, entered service in the 1930s, and were the most notable examples of this aerodynamically unrefined tendency. Yet even these French machines appeared modern in comparison with a British contemporary, the Handley Page Heyford – a large biplane with the fuselage attached to the underside of the upper wing and the bomb load stowed in the thick centre section of the lower wing.

Meanwhile, fighters remained little more advanced in concept than World War I types. The first such machines to enter service with the RAF after the war were the Armstrong Whitworth Siskin and the Gloster Grebe, both of which made their service debuts in 1924. Several companies produced experimental monoplane fighters during the decade following the

The Martin B-10 was the American warplane that opened the era of the 'modern' monoplane bomber with features such as its metal structure, cantilever wing, enclosed accommodation, turreted nose armament, wing-mounted engines in stylish low-drag cowlings, and retractable main landing gear units. The B-10B was ordered in 1934, and its data include an offensive armament of 2,260lb (1,025kg) of bombs carried in the large ventral weapons bay, a defensive armament of three 0.3in (7.62mm) Browning trainable machine-guns, a powerplant of two 775hp Wright R-1820-33 air-cooled radial engines, a maximum speed of 213mph (343km/h) at optimum altitude, a ceiling of 24,200ft (7,375m), a range of 1,240 miles (1996km), empty and maximum take-off weights of 9,681 and 16,400lb (4391 and 7,439kg) respectively, span of 70ft 6in (21.49m) and length of 44ft 9in (13.64m).

war, but the RAF rigidly adhered to the well-proved biplane formula, usually with a radial engine, for a period of some 15 years after World War I. Later types such as the Bristol Bulldog, Gloster Gauntlet and Gloster Gladiator continued this tradition, and the only notable exception was the Hawker Fury. Powered by a Rolls-Royce Kestrel inline piston engine, this was the first British fighter to exceed 200mph (320km/h) in level flight.

Keynotes of the design philosophy that created these fighters were the strong yet light biplane layout, the excellent manoeuvrability, and the armament of two rifle-calibre machine-guns located with their breeches within easy reach of the pilot, who could thus solve the problem of jammed rounds. British light bombers followed the same basic formula, but carried a gunner behind the pilot and a small bomb load under the lower wings. Classic examples were the Fairey Fox, Hawker Hart and Hawker Hind. The major difference between all these aircraft and their counterparts in World War I was the widespread use of metal in the structures of the later machines. This use of metal became Air Ministry policy after 1924, to avoid the problems encountered in World War I through shortage of suitably seasoned timber for airframes, and gradually became more common in other parts of British military aircraft, but as the basic design philosophy remained unaltered, the aircraft were essentially wooden types rendered in metal.

Although often condemned for being 'behind the times' in the 1920s and 1930s, the French were well up with the leaders in the field of fighters. Several advanced monoplane designs were evolved during the 1920s, with heavily braced parasol or gull wings. These offered strength, relatively low drag and a good field of vision for the pilot. Unlike the British, many of whose aircraft companies had disappeared in the troubled times after the war, the French could rely on long-established firms such as Morane-Saulnier, Nieuport and SPAD, as well as more recent companies such as Dewoitine, Loire and Wibault. The 1920s, therefore, saw a large number of interesting fighters, and a smaller number of reconnaissance and light bomber machines, which were being offered both for the home market and for export sale.

In the late 1920s and early 1930s, the French aircraft industry revealed a strong penchant for extraordinarily slab-sided bombers with angular flying surfaces, massive fixed landing gear units, and excrescences such as balconied gun/bombing positions and observation gondolas. The result was aircraft that were comparatively easy to make, but possessed so high a drag factor that their performance was severely compromised even with moderately powerful engines. A good example of this tendency is the Bloch MB.200 heavy bomber that entered service in 1934 and was still in limited service in the first stages of World War II. This could carry a bomb load of 5,511lb (2,500kg) and was defended by three 0.295in (7.5mm) trainable machines guns and, with a powerplant of two 870hp Gnome-Rhône 14Kirs/Kjrs air-cooled radial engines, could attain a maximum speed of 143mph (230km/h), a ceiling of 26,245ft (8,000m) and a normal range of 621 miles (1,000km). The MB.200 had a maximum take-off weight of 16,050lb (7,280kg), and its dimensions included a span of 73ft 7.67in (22.45m) and length of 52ft 6in (16.00m).

Fighter Armament

DURING World War I, the standard fixed forward-firing armament for fighters had started in 1915 as one rifle-calibre machine-gun synchronised to fire through the propeller disc, and by 1917 had been standardised as two such weapons. This weight of fire was adequate during the time and through most of the 1920s, and the weapons were usually located in the fuselage so that the pilot could reach the breeches and clear the jammed rounds that were common with the ammunition of the period. The sole major exception to this tendency were the Americans, who made provision for one of the two rifle-calibre weapons to be replaced by a heavy machine-gun of 0.5in (12.7mm) calibre for heavier weight of fire to a longer range.

During the later 1920s, however, the performance of warplanes started to improve so rapidly as a result of the adoption of more powerful engines, improved aerodynamics and more advanced structural practices, that many air forces began to query the continued efficacy of the two machine-guns as the armament of fighters designed to tackle larger and more sturdily constructed bombers whose high performance meant that they could be kept in the sights of intercepting fighters for only fleeting moments. This suggested not only the development of more advanced fighters (leading to the introduction of the 'modern' fighter with a cantilever low-set wing, enclosed cockpit and retractable main landing gear units) but to consideration of heavier armament.

By the mid-1930s, this heavier armament was seen as taking the form of the same number of larger-calibre weapons or alternatively a larger number of weapons of the same calibre. The former offered greater striking power per round (including explosive shells if the 20mm cannon was adopted) but a smaller number of rounds as the larger-calibre weapons could not match the firing rate of rifle-calibre machine-guns), while the latter offered the possibility of swamping the target with a mass of relatively light rounds. Most European air forces opted for a mixed battery of cannon and rifle-calibre machine-guns (typically one 20mm cannon and two or four rifle-calibre machine-guns), the British decided to increase the number of rifle-calibre machine-guns to four and then eight pending the development of the cannon to a more capable standard, and the Americans opted generally for a battery of two heavy and four rifle-calibre machines guns evolving rapidly to six or even eight heavy machine-guns for a combination of a high volume of fire with a round that offered considerably greater striking power than the rifle-calibre round. Of the other major aeronautical powers, the USSR opted for the combination of one 20mm cannon and a mixed machine-gun battery and then for a larger number of cannon, while Japan was divided, the Imperial Japanese army air force remained a believer in relatively light armament (just two rifle-calibre or heavy machine-guns) up to a fairly late date, and the Imperial Japanese army air force was an early adherent to the concept of heavier firepower in the form of two 20mm cannon and a number of rifle-calibre or heavy machine-guns.

At the end of the 1920s, the French air force was equipped with the parasol-winged Nieuport-Delage NiD.62 series, the Loire/Gourdou-Leseurre 32 and the Wibault 72, all capable of a maximum speed in the order of 260km/h (160mph). In 1930, however, the French realised that all its fighters were approaching obsolescence, and so issued specifications for a new standard fighter. The best response came from the Dewoitine company, which had experimented with a number of sturdy parasol types in the 1920's and had won a good export record. For its D.500 series Dewoitine adopted a new layout: a cantilever low-wing monoplane powered by a closely cowled Hispano-Suiza 12Y inline piston engine (soon to become the most important French aero engine of the decade), and supported on the ground by wide-track fixed landing gear. The new fighter had a top speed of 360km/h (225mph), which was far higher than the maximum speeds of current first-line French fighters.

The United States, on the other hand, was at last beginning to emerge from the aeronautical wilderness into which it had fallen during the middle of the 1920s. The gradual development of the fledgling commercial airlines was partially responsible for this renaissance, but equally significant was the amalgamation of a number of small builders into a few large and increasingly well-organised concerns, each operating in a custom-built, modern factory accommodating design staff, experimental workshops and production lines. Pratt & Whitney and Wright had become the two most important and competitive aero engine manufacturers, and these two major companies were producing reliable air-cooled radials such as the Pratt & Whitney Wasp and its derivatives, and the Wright Whirlwind and

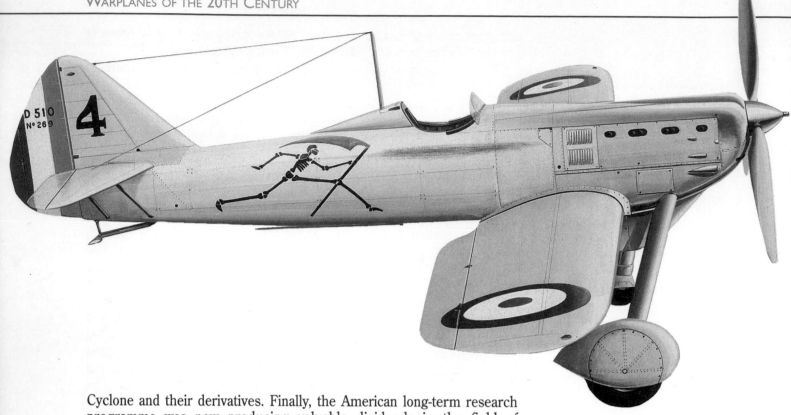

Cyclone and their derivatives. Finally, the American long-term research programme was now producing valuable dividends in the field of structures and aerodynamics.

The American revival became fully evident with the advent of a number of new and formidable aircraft produced in the late 1920s and early 1930s. The Boeing B-9 and Martin B-10 bombers mentioned above were two clear examples of advanced aerodynamic theory allied to advanced military concepts, but the fighter equipment of the two American air forces also revealed that the American aeronautical machine now possessed strength in depth. The US Army and the US Navy each had its own air force, with the US Marine Corps operating further air formations flying basically the same types of aircraft as the US Navy.

Authorities in most countries with aspirations of naval air power, principally the United Kingdom, felt that the complex requirements of carrierborne operations meant that naval aircraft had to embody a compromise between several design factors, and therefore could not be a match for land-based aircraft. The US Navy, on the other hand, realised that its carriers would play a dominant part in any future war, principally because of the geographical isolation of the United States between the Pacific and Atlantic oceans. It was therefore crucial that the aircraft-carrier arm's aircraft were capable of combating land-based aircraft. The early realisation of this fact proved highly significant in America's struggle with Japan from 1941 onwards.

The most important carrierborne fighters of the US Navy were the Curtiss Hawk and Boeing F2B, each possessing a maximum speed of 155mph (250km/h), later supplanted by the Boeing F4B, which was capable of 190mph (305km/h). The US Army Air Corps' fighters of the period were the Boeing PW-9 and Curtiss P-6, capable of 155 and 180mph (250 and 318km/h) respectively, later joined by the Boeing P-12 (the land plane equivalent of the F4B), and in 1933 by the Boeing P-26 'Peashooter', the first American monoplane fighter, which was capable of 235mph (380km/h). Of these only the P-26 represented an extraordinary advance on its predecessors, but all these fighters were workmanlike aircraft notable for their sturdy construction, high manoeuvrability and good performance.

Despite its belief (or perhaps suspension of disbelief) in angularity for its larger warplanes during the later 1920s and early 1930s, France was considerably more adventurous in the design of fighters, and as such was a pioneer of the monoplane fighter in a number of different configurations. One of the most important of these, which entered service in 1935 and was still in limited service at the time of France's defeat by Germany in June 1940, was the Dewoitine D.500. This was of all-metal construction with a cantilever low-set wing, but cannot be regarded as truly modern as it retained an open pilot's cockpit and fixed landing gear. The D.500 was powered by one 600hp Hispano-Suiza 12Xbrs water-cooled engine, and the armament comprised one 20mm cannon (located between the engine's two cylinder banks to fire through the hollow propeller shaft) and two 0.295in (7.5mm) machine-guns installed in the wing leading edges. The D.500 could attain a maximum speed of 224mph (360km/h) at optimum altitude, and its other primary performance data included a ceiling of 34,450ft (10,500m) and a range of 528 miles (850km). The type had a maximum take-off weight of 3,770lb (1,710kg), and its dimensional data included a span of 39ft 8in (12.10m) and length of 25ft 4.75in (7.74m).

Although they had no long pedigree, therefore, they were in most respects the equals of contemporary British and French fighters.

The development of aircraft had not yet become prohibitively expensive, so it was normal for all but the very poorest countries to try their hand at the design and production of fighters and other small aircraft. Most notable of these was the Polish PZL P.7 fighter of 1932. An inverted gull-wing monoplane clearly inspired by French design thinking, the P.7 was powered by a licence-built Bristol Jupiter radial, and capable of 200mph (320km/h). Further development led to the P.11 and P.24, both of which performed well in the hands of Polish and Greek pilots against the Luftwaffe in 1939 and 1941.

Yugoslavia and Czechoslovakia were also building fighters in this period, and some mention must also be made of Italy. Although not a poor country, Italy had gone into an aeronautical slump in the late 1920s, despite her excellent seaplanes and heroic efforts in the Schneider Trophy races. Not until 1933, with the development of the Fiat CR.32, did all Italian combat aircraft reach world standards. Designed by the illustrious Celestino Rosatelli, the CR.32 was very strong and manoeuvrable, and it was fast for its time, with a top speed of 370km/h (230mph). The very capabilities of the CR.32 led to unfortunate consequences for the Italians, however: so good was the CR.32 that little notice was taken of the rapidly advancing theory of air warfare, and accordingly no priority was given to the development of an advanced successor.

By 1933, therefore, the design philosophies of World War I had been completely revised. There were still believers in the biplane formula, including the Italians, but this design concept's practical limits had been reached by fighters such as the Gloster Gladiator from the United Kingdom, the Fiat CR.42 from Italy, and the Polikarpov I-153 from the USSR.

Even before this, however, the nature and shape of the biplane's inevitable successor had been demonstrated by the Boeing and Martin bombers, the French monoplane fighters, and the racing aircraft developed by the United Kingdom, Italy and the United States. The high-drag biplane with fixed landing gear was to be supplanted by the low-drag monoplane with retractable landing gear. This change had already begun when the

The main rival to Boeing and Douglas for the supply of warplanes to the US services in the late 1920s and early 1930s was Curtiss, which designed and manufactured a number of classic warplane types. One of the most important of these, which has perhaps never received the full credit that is due to it, is the Falcon series of biplanes that was produced in three basic forms for service from 1927 as the A-3 for the land-based attack role, F8C for the carrierborne fighter and fighter-bomber roles, and the O-1 and O-11 for the land-based observation and reconnaissance roles. The aeroplane seen here is an O-1, and the data for the two-seat O-1E may be taken as typical for the type: powered by one 435hp Curtiss V-1150-5 Conqueror liquid-cooled engine and armed with four 0.3in (7.62mm) Browning machine-guns (two fixed and two trainable), this model attained a maximum speed of 141mph (227km/h) at optimum altitude, an initial climb rate of 980ft (299m) per minute, and a ceiling of 15,300ft (4,665m); the type had empty and maximum take-off weights of 2,922 and 4,347lb (1,325 and 1,972kg) respectively, and its primary dimensional data included a span of 38ft 0in (11.58m) and length of 27ft 2in (8.28m).

process was boosted by the reappearance of Germany on the military scene.

With the connivance of Sweden and the USSR, Germany had circumvented the clauses of the Treaty of Versailles which prohibited its development of advanced offensive weapons. In both these countries German designers had been free to plan and build military aircraft and tanks, and in Germany itself fighters and bombers had appeared in the guise of sporting planes and airliners. A clandestine air force had been prepared under cover of the air ministry, the national airline and various flying clubs that had been formed all over Germany.

In 1935, Adolf Hitler announced Germany's renunciation of the military terms of the Treaty of Versailles, and a fully fledged Luftwaffe was unveiled overnight. This force possessed a large number of aircraft and also enjoyed the backing of a powerful aircraft industry together with a large number of well-planned and well-staffed military airfields.

At first the Luftwaffe was not equipped with particularly advanced aircraft, the standard fighter and bomber being the Heinkel He 51 biplane and Junkers Ju 52/3m monoplane respectively. Knowing that military operations were still probably some distance in the future, the Luftwaffe

An odd and angular little aeroplane, but one possessing beautiful handling characteristics and excellent agility, the Fairey Flycatcher was the most important carrierborne fighter operated by the British from 1923 into the early 1930s before finally disappearing from service in 1935. The Flycatcher was powered by one 400hp Armstrong Siddeley Jaguar II or IV air-cooled radial engine and was armed with two 0.303in (7.7mm) Vickers fixed forward-firing and synchronised machine-guns. The type's performance included a maximum speed of 134mph (216km/h) at 5,000ft (1,525m), a ceiling of 20,600ft (6,280m) and a range of 310 miles (499km), its maximum take-off weight was 2,979lb (1,351kg), and its dimensional data included a span of 29ft 0in (8.84m) and length of 23ft 0in (7.01m).

high command was satisfied with these aircraft as 'operational' trainers which, in the period before the advent of more advanced aircraft, could suffice as 'front-line' machines. Newer types were already being designed or placed in production, and it was these aircraft that would establish the Luftwaffe as an extraordinarily potent exponent of tactical air power in the first campaigns of World War II.

Exaggerated claims for the Luftwaffe have helped to obscure the great advances made by the USSR in the late 1920s and early 1930s. After experimenting with strategic heavy bombing from aircraft such as the Tupolev ANT-6, and causing a number of aeronautical eyebrows to be raised as a result of its long-distance record breaking aircraft, the USSR decided that the most important role for air power was tactical support of ground forces. A new generation of tactical aircraft was developed, based on the latest advances in aeronautical techniques. The Soviets also built competitive aircraft, pressing the limits of current experimental concepts so that the widest spectrum of aeronautical and structural notions could be tested.

One of the earliest and most important results of this Soviet programme was the 1934 appearance of the Polikarpov I-16, which has the distinction of being the world's first cantilever low-wing monoplane fighter with retractable landing gear. The first examples of this epoch-making type also possessed another advanced feature in the form of an enclosed cockpit, but pilots did not like this enclosure and it was eliminated from later variants. The 700hp (522kW) radial engine was mounted in a very bluff, high-drag nose, but this notwithstanding, the I-16 could attain 280mph (450km/h), comparing very favourably with the maximum speed of 223mph (359km/h) attained by the Gloster Gauntlet which appeared in the following year. The Soviet programme then seemed to relax, and the German invasion six years later found the Soviet fighter arm still equipped mainly with later models of the I-16, and even large numbers of the I-15bis and I-153 biplane fighters.

The country which then took the practical lead in introducing advanced combat aircraft was Germany. After lengthy evaluation, the Messerschmitt Bf 109 was selected as the Luftwaffe's primary fighter, the Dornier Do 17 and Heinkel He 111 as its standard medium bombers, and the Junkers Ju 87 Stuka (abbreviated from *Sturzkampfflugzeug*, or dive-bomber) as its basic tactical support aeroplane.

The last of the Luftwaffe's mainstay aircraft to appear before World War II was the Junkers Ju 88 medium bomber, which entered service in 1939. The Ju 88 was originally intended as a fast medium bomber with limited dive-bombing capability, but served with great distinction in a variety of roles throughout World War II. In terms of versatility, the Ju 88 was rivalled only by the remarkable British de Havilland D.H.98 Mosquito.

The Germans tested the standard European concept of air power during the Spanish Civil War (1936-39). German aircraft were involved from the beginning, when Ju 52/3m transports were used to ferry General Francisco Franco's Nationalist troops from Spanish Morocco into southern Spain. As a bomber, however, the Ju 52/3m proved a failure, as did the Heinkel He 51 fighter when opposed by the formidable Soviet I-15 and I-16 fighters.

As the latest German combat aircraft emerged from their production lines they were sent to Spain in small numbers for operational evaluation. It was here that most of Germany's early World War II aircraft first saw combat and pilots learned how to get the best out of their aircraft. The problems with German aircraft in combat were experienced and cured, and as a result the Luftwaffe was a confident and experienced air force by the start of World War II in 1939.

Lessons of the Spanish Civil War

FOUGHT between 1936 and 1939, the Spanish Civil War pitted the Nationalist insurgent movement against the Republican government, the former with the active aid of the Germans and Italians, and the latter with the support of the USSR. Though these three countries backed the ideological aims of the Spanish side they supported, they also had a number of less altruistic reasons for their involvement in this bitter war, which was eventually won by the Nationalists. These reasons included the operational evaluation of modern weapons under harsh combat conditions, and the testing of their latest tactical and operational thinking.

The USSR sent examples of its most modern warplanes to Spain, including the Polikarpov I-15 and I-16 fighters and the Tupolev SB-2 bomber, and in the light of experience in this theatre decided that there was continued viability in a two-handed approach to fighter design (the monoplane for high-speed interception and the more agile biplane for air combat), but that considerations of strategic air power should be forsaken for complete concentration on tactical air power for the support of the ground forces, which were deemed to be the decisive element of the Soviet armed forces. The Italian experience was basically similar to that of the USSR, certainly as far as the two-handed approach to fighter design was concerned.

Germany also decided that the most important lesson of the Spanish Civil War was the creation of an air force optimised for tactical operations, and as a result effectively ceased development of long-range heavy warplanes in place of attack aircraft and multi-role medium bombers. Contrary to the Soviet and Italian conclusion, however, Germany decided that the day of the biplane fighter was clearly over, and henceforward concentrated its fighter developments on the modern monoplane fighter.

The results of this thinking became evident in World War II (1939-45), when German tactical air power was a decisive element in the success of German arms up to 1942, but was thereafter revealed as wholly inadequate to stem the tide of Allied and Soviet air power once earlier misconceptions had been set aside and more advanced aircraft were being produced in an ever swelling tide.

The Germans entered the Spanish Civil War with a firm belief in using their aircraft in a strategic role, but soon discovered the vulnerability of their bombers when these were forced to operate without long-range fighter escort. After the death in a 1936 flying accident of Lieutenant-General Walther Wever, the Luftwaffe's first chief-of-staff and Germany's primary protagonist of strategic air power, the Germans effectively turned their backs on the concept of strategic bombing and devoted virtually their full attention to the development of tactical air power to be used as 'flying artillery' in support of the German army's new fast-moving, hard-hitting armoured divisions. Thus the Luftwaffe became a tactical air force in terms

Above: Of all-metal construction with a skinning of corrugated Dural alloy, the Tupolev ANT-5 entered service in 1928 as the I-4 single-seat fighter, and for its time was a very advanced type with a sesquiplane wing cellule. The I-4 was powered by one 460hp M-22 (licence-built Bristol Jupiter) air-cooled radial engine, and was armed with two 0.3in (7.62mm) fixed forward-firing and synchronised machine-guns. The type's performance included a maximum speed of 160mph (258km/h) at optimum altitude and a ceiling of 25,100ft (7,650m), its maximum take-off weight was 3,000lb (1,360kg), and its dimensions included a span of 37ft 5in (11.40m) and length of 23ft 10.5in (7.28m).

Opposite: Produced in both landplane and floatplane forms (above and below respectively), the Heinkel He 51 was one of Germany's last single-seat biplane fighters, and as such marked one of the high points in the design of such warplanes even though it was obsolescent as it entered service in 1934. The definitive He 51B-1 was powered by one 750hp BMW VI water-cooled engine and armed with two 0.312in (7.92mm) MG17 fixed forward-firing and synchronised machine-guns, and its performance included a maximum speed of 205mph (330km/h) at optimum altitude, a ceiling of 25,350ft (7725m) and a range of 431 miles (695km). The type had a maximum take-off weight of 4,189lb (1,900kg), and its dimensional data included a span of 36ft 1.5in (11.00m) and a length of 27ft 6.75in (8.40m).

of its equipment, practical experience, training and operational philosophy.

The initial successes enjoyed by the Axis powers (Germany, Italy and Japan) were partially due to the fact that all three nations had gained experience before the outbreak of World War II. Italy had not only supported the Nationalists in Spain, but had also been able to test her forces in the conquest of Abyssinia, which began in 1935. The Italian bombers, principally the Savoia-Marchetti S.M.79 tri-motor monoplane, distinguished themselves in Spain, but the CR.32 and CR.42 fighters appeared better than they were, due to their phenomenal agility.

The Italian Regia Aeronautica therefore emerged from these two campaigns overestimating the operational utility of its first-line fighters. Three very promising designs for monoplane fighters, the Fiat G.50 Freccia, Macchi MC.200 Saetta and Reggiane Re.2000 Sagittario, were developed just before World War II, but the Italians had failed to keep up with the development of high-powered inline engines. All three of these potentially good fighters were therefore fitted with low-powered radials: furthermore, speed and rate of climb were also sacrificed to the pilots' expressed preference for manoeuvrability. Armament was poor, especially compared with the standards set in German fighters, which had 20mm cannon firing explosive shells.

Like Germany, Japan came late to modern aviation, and developed a good air force almost from the beginning. Although the army and navy had possessed their own air arms since 1911, Japan began to develop her aircraft industries and air forces only in the 1930s. Content at first to build Western types under licence, so absorbing the latest production and design techniques, Japan began a major expansion of her air forces in the mid-1930s, using her own designs.

The Western nations were only too glad to condemn these Japanese aircraft as inferior copies and adaptations of Western designs. In fact, they were skilfully designed to take advantage of Japan's capacity for producing lightweight structures with heavy armament, superior agility and good

43

performance especially in speed, climb rate and range. The Mitsubishi A5M and Nakajima Ki-27 low-wing monoplane fighters had very good performance despite their retention of fixed landing gear arrangements, and the next generation of fighters was even better. The Mitsubishi A6M Reisen (zero fighter), later known as the 'Zeke', received a glowing assessment from Americans flying against them in China, as did the Mitsubishi G3M 'Nell' and G4M 'Betty' bombers. All such warnings were disregarded, and this was to cost the Allies dearly in 1941 and 1942.

By 1936 the United Kingdom and France had become thoroughly alarmed by the nature and rate of German military expansion, and decided to institute major rearmament programmes in which aircraft had a high priority. The nationalised French aircraft groups created during 1936 in the north, centre, west, south-west and south-east of the country had produced some excellent designs by the beginning of the war, but these were not ready in time for the French campaign of 1940. The main burden fell instead on aircraft designed by the few successful private firms: Dewoitine's petite D.520 fighter, Morane-Saulnier's angular M.S.406 fighter, Bloch's stubby but powerful MB.151 fighter, Breguet's promising Bre.690 twin-engined fighter and Potez's useful Type 63 twin-engined fighter-bomber. Other excellent machines that could have played an important role had more of them been delivered in time were the Bloch MB.175 light bomber, the elegant Lioré-et-Olivier LeO 451 medium bomber and the useful Amiot 350 series bomber.

By the middle of the 1930s the British aircraft industry was well advanced in the production of important new fighters: the RAF abandoned the biplane formula after the Gloster Gladiator and turned to the low-wing monoplane. The best-known of these were the Hawker Hurricane and the Supermarine

A Fairey Flycatcher fighter flies past the British aircraft-carrier HMS Eagle during the 1930s. This was a time of great and rapid change in the nature of maritime air capabilities as the more important naval powers replaced their early-generation carrierborne warplanes with more advanced monoplanes offering considerably higher performance.

Spitfire, each powered by the magnificent Rolls-Royce Merlin engine and armed with eight rifle-calibre machine-guns. Both these interceptors had top speeds in the order of 350mph (565km/h), about 100mph (160km/h) faster than the Gladiator. With their retractable landing gear, trailing-edge flaps and enclosed cockpits, the aircraft caused problems at first in operational units, but as soon as pilots had mastered the necessary techniques the Hurricane and Spitfire won great popularity.

The British bomber force was also given completely new equipment in the shape of the Armstrong Whitworth Whitley, the Handley Page Hampden and the Vickers Wellington, each of these being cantilever low-wing monoplane bombers with twin engines and retractable landing gear. There was also the Fairey Battle single-engined light bomber, which was to prove almost worthless in combat, and the twin-engined Bristol Blenheim light bomber, an advanced and speedy aeroplane for its time, although somewhat flimsy and under-armed.

The Americans were producing some very advanced aircraft, including the first Boeing B-17 Flying Fortress four-engined heavy bomber in 1935, but they still lagged behind the Europeans in the theory and practice of air warfare. American aircraft had good performance, and allowed the pilot to perform his tasks in some comfort, but they lacked the 'edge' of their European counterparts. Nonetheless, American production was considerable, and the European powers were happy to order large quantities of aircraft such as the Curtiss P-36 and P-40 fighters, the Douglas DB-7 and Martin Maryland bombers, and a number of other types. Meanwhile, the Americans were hard at work on a new generation of aircraft that would make great and enduring reputations for themselves in World War II.

The Supermarine Spitfire may be regarded as the UK's first truly 'modern' fighter of the 1930s, for it was of metal construction with a stressed-skin metal covering and incorporated 'modern' features such as an enclosed cockpit, a cantilever low-set wing, retractable main landing gear units, trailing-edge flaps and, in the definitive models, a propeller of the variable-pitch type. The slightly earlier Hawker Hurricane, on the other hand, was not truly a 'modern' fighter as it had an earlier-generation structure based on steel tube covered with fabric.

During this period, both British and German scientists had been working on a new type of powerplant that would revolutionise aircraft design and operation. This was the turbojet engine, which was intended to thrust the aeroplane forward by the reaction of a stream of gases flowing backwards. Frank Whittle's early prototype ran for the first time in April 1937, and Hans von Ohain's model a month later. These British and German pioneers were working entirely independently of each other and evolved radically different types of engine. In fact, the Germans soon overtook the British, and scored a considerable success when in August 1939, less than one week before the outbreak of World War II, the Heinkel He 178 became the world's first jet-powered aeroplane to fly. Yet the authorities in both Germany and the United Kingdom were slow to appreciate the possibilities of such engines, and operational jet aircraft did not appear until late in World War II.

World War II in the Air

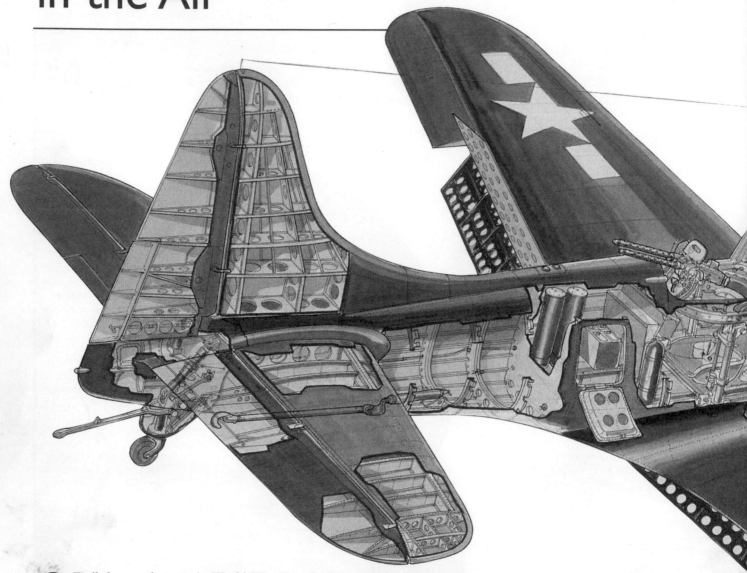

OF all the combatants in World War II, only Germany had evolved a practical method of tactical air support for its ground forces in the period leading up to hostilities. Careful evaluation of their performance in the Spanish Civil War had led the Germans to work out a new system of warfare in which the main striking elements were the armoured forces and their tactical air support formations. Contrary to popular belief, the German armed forces at the start of World War II did not comprise vast formations of tanks and infantry, mechanised and homogeneous, supported by masses of aircraft. In reality, the German formations were on the whole rather old-fashioned, relying heavily on horse transport and cumbersome artillery. The strength of the German army for offensive operations, however, lay in the relatively small but well-trained *Panzer* (tank) divisions.

The role of the Panzer formations was to strike swiftly and deeply into the enemy's defences, isolating his main operational groupings both from each other and the high command, and as a result destroying his cohesion in military, political and economic terms. As the Panzer forces bit deep into hostile territory, relying on mobility to keep them out of trouble, the infantry would follow up more slowly, completing the isolation of enemy groups, 'mopping up' and consolidating in the wake of the Panzer formations.

In theory this was a neat and economical solution to the question of how best to avoid the type of static warfare that had become the norm during World War I. As the Germans had discovered in Spain, however, the practical reality was that the Panzer formations could not fulfil their task on their own as they lacked the heavy fire support so frequently needed. Artillery would have been the conventional answer, but the German artillery was neither modern nor mobile enough to keep up with the Panzer formations. The solution was found in deployment of the Luftwaffe

Douglas SBD Dauntless

THE Douglas SBD Dauntless was the most important dive-bomber operated by the US Navy and US Marine Corps in the first half of World War II. Although it was at best obsolescent by 1944 in terms of its primary anti-ship role, the type was retained in service because of the limitations of its successor, the Curtiss SB2C Helldiver, and operated from the smaller escort (or 'jeep') carriers for the support of amphibious landings in the later stages of World War II. Rugged and reliable, the Dauntless was well liked by its crews for these primary features as well as its adequate performance and considerable agility. Total production was 5,937 aircraft in a number of variants characterised by heavier armament, increased fuel capacity, enhanced defensive features (improved armour protection and self-sealing fuel tanks), and an uprated engine. The Dauntless was used by France, New Zealand, Mexico and the UK in addition to the USA, although the British aircraft were used for training rather than combat, and the Mexican aircraft were limited in operational terms to anti-submarine patrols in the Gulf of Mexico.

With 3,025 built, the SBD-5 was the last major production version and may be taken as a good representative of the type. The SBD had a crew of two (pilot and observer/gunner), was powered by one Wright R-1820-60 Cyclone air-cooled radial piston engine rated at 1,200hp, and carried a disposable armament of 2,250lb (1,021kg) in the form of a 1,600lb (726kg) or smaller bomb on the underfuselage crutch used to swing the bomb clear of the propeller before release, and 650lb (295kg) of smaller bombs under the wings; the gun armament comprised two 0.5in (12.7mm) fixed forward-firing machine guns operated by the pilot, and two 0.3in (7.62mm) trainable rearward-firing machine guns operated buy the observer/gunner. The SBD-5's other primary details included a span of 41ft 6.25in (12,65m), length of 33ft 0in (1,0.06m), empty weight of 6,533lb (2,963kg), maximum take-off weight of 10,700lb (4,855kg), maximum speed of 245mph (394km/h) at 15,800ft (4,815m), initial climb rate of 1,190ft (363m) per minute, service ceiling of 24,300ft (7,405m), and range of 1,100 miles (1,770km).

47

for this task. Under the command of Hermann Göring, a World War I air ace, the Luftwaffe quickly evolved as a highly mobile and efficient tactical support force.

Effective co-operation between the ground and air forces was essential for the success of the new *Blitzkrieg* (lightning war) tactics, and this co-operation was wholly dependent on radio communications, which were assured by allocating a number of air controllers in specially equipped half-track vehicles to all the major combat units as well as to senior commanders. If a Panzer battalion ran into stiff resistance, it could call for air support without suffering the inevitable delay of going through a higher command echelon. The value of these forward controllers, able to speak directly to the air units, played a significant part in Germany's successes in 1939 and 1940.

Tactical support for the army appeared complex because of the large number of different types of aircraft involved. It was in fact a smooth and relatively simple affair, with each type of aeroplane playing an individual and specific role. Far forward of the actual fighting, for instance, operational reconnaissance aircraft, usually converted bombers carrying a number of cameras, kept constant watch for any signs of enemy activity that might have an important long-term effect on the campaign.

Over the battlefield itself, and just forward of it, tactical reconnaissance machines such as the Fieseler Fi 156 Storch kept a watchful eye on short-term developments. Providing short-range cover for these aircraft, and also supporting the ground forces with machine-gun and cannon fire, were the single-engined Messerschmitt Bf 109 fighters. Also available in comparatively large numbers was the twin-engined Messerschmitt Bf 110

The Fieseler Fi 156 Storch was Germany's most important battlefield liaison aeroplane of World War II, and was also operated in the battlefield observation role. The type's most important characteristic was its phenomenally good low-speed handling as a result of its low wing loading and the high-lift devices on the leading and trailing edges of its wing. This produced exceptionally good field performance of the short take-off and landing (STOL) type, and also allowed the aeroplane virtually to hover in only modest winds.

Zerstörer (destroyer) heavy fighter, whose primary function was to hunt down enemy bombers, but which could also support the ground forces with machine-gun and cannon fire. A dedicated ground-attack aeroplane, the single-engined Henschel Hs 123 biplane, with fixed landing gear, was used only in the war's early campaigns: its offensive complement of machine-guns and light bombs, brought to bear accurately by the aeroplane's steadiness and considerable low-level agility, made it very useful against enemy infantry.

The dread of most enemy infantry, however, was the Junkers Ju 87 Stuka dive-bomber, which was used to provide the Panzer units with extremely accurate support at close ranges, thus replacing conventional horse- and tractor-drawn artillery. The Stukas were armed with bombs up to 500kg (1,102lb) in weight, and were capable of dealing with most of the enemy's defensive positions and tanks. Finally, support of a more general nature was provided by Dornier Do 17, Heinkel He 111 and Junkers Ju 88 medium bombers, which could operate at low level, and therefore with greater accuracy, once the Bf 109s had eliminated the enemy's air cover.

Battlefield support of this type was the Luftwaffe's main task, but it depended first on the destruction of the enemy's air power, usually by attacks on the enemy's main airfields at the start of hostilities. Undertaken

In numerical terms the Messerschmitt Bf 109 was Germany's most important fighter of World War II, and in 1939 and 1940 was in real terms her only single-engined fighter until supplemented by the superlative Focke-Wulf Fw 190 multi-role fighter. Illustrated here is an example of the Bf 109E-3, one of the standard fighters used by the Luftwaffe in the Battle of Britain. Powered by a Daimler-Benz DB 601Aa liquid-cooled inverted-Vee piston engine, the Bf 109E-3 was armed with two 20mm MG FF fixed forward-firing cannon in the wing leading edges, two 0.312in (7.92mm) MG 17 fixed forward-firing machine guns in the upper part of the forward fuselage and, on some aircraft, one 20 mm MG FF/M fixed forward-firing cannon located between the engine cylinder banks to fire through the hollow propeller shaft. The Bf 109E-3 had a maximum speed of 348mph (560km/h) at 14,560ft (4,440m), and among its attributes was the ability to nose straight down into a dive without the fuel-injected engine cutting out.

on a large scale by the medium bombers, such raids were truly devastating and generally caused such destruction that airfields were rendered inoperative, with comparatively few combat aircraft likely to have survived the bombers' attentions. While the bombers roamed deep into the enemy's rear areas to destroy airfields, turning their attentions to targets such as transport and communications centres, the German fighters attacked their counterparts in the air during the first few days of the campaign. The success of this operational method is attested by the fact that in their first campaigns, the Germans encountered virtually no significant air opposition

First tested with considerable success in the Spanish Civil War, the Junkers Ju 87 dive-bomber was universally known as the 'Stuka' and in the first campaigns of World War II proved an invaluable asset for the Germans in the course of their campaigns of conquest in Poland, North-West Europe, and the Balkans. Here the Ju 87 was not faced by significant fighter or anti-aircraft artillery opposition, and was therefore able to operate effectively in its role of 'flying artillery' for the Panzer divisions, blasting any defensive feature that might have hindered the rapid progress of these armoured formations. The Battle of Britain highlighted the tactical limitations of the Ju 87 against a high-grade defence, however, and the Ju 87 was then translated into a potent if limited anti-tank type such as this Ju 87G with a pair of 37mm cannon under the wings

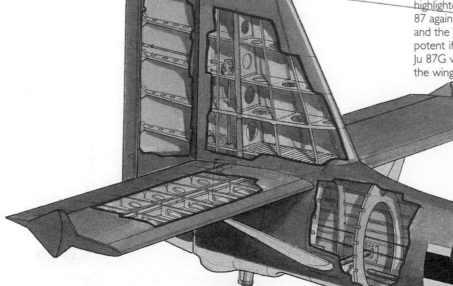

after the first few hours or days of any campaign, and this allowed the bulk of their tactical air strength to be allocated to the direct support of the ground forces.

The Ju 87 was central to the German concept of tactical support. A very sturdy aeroplane with wide-track fixed landing gear, the Stuka could operate from rough airstrips close behind the front line, allowing it to make frequent sorties and to respond rapidly to calls for close support. The aeroplane's performance was adequate and its offensive load quite good by the standards of the day, making it an effective combat type.

Yet a large part of the Stuka's success was due to its psychological effect. The angular Ju 87 had a belligerent and aggressive aspect, most impressive as it dived under full control – assisted by the powerful and effective dive-brakes under its wings, and this aspect was enhanced by the screaming of the pair of 'Jericho trumpets' installed as single units in each landing gear fairing. These emitted a banshee howl of increasing pitch as the Stuka swooped down to release its bombs only a few hundred feet above the target. The combination of the Stuka's appearance and sound, and later its reputation, did much to demoralise opposing ground forces during 1939 and 1940.

The Polish campaign which opened World War II began on 1 September 1939, and the Luftwaffe soon proved its worth. The Polish air force fought back, using combat aircraft such as the single-engined P.11

Junkers Ju 87 'Stuka'

BUILT to a total of 5,709 aircraft up to 1944, when it was finally phased out of production despite the fact that it had no successor, the Ju 87 was an extremely sturdy aeroplane able to undertake nearly vertical attacks for the delivery of its bomb load with pinpoint accuracy. The speed in the dive was controlled by powerful air brakes under the wings, and recovery from the dive was made under control of an automatic system as the high g loadings of the recovery tended to cause the pilot to black out. The fear of the Ju 87's accurate attack was further enhanced by the 'Jericho trumpets' in the main landing gear legs: the increasing pitch of these sirens as the Ju 87 dived became a potent morale-shattering weapon in its own right against poorly trained troops.

The Ju 87B-1 may be taken as typical of the 'Stuka' in its primary dive-bomber form. The type was manned by a pilot and a radio operator/gunner in tandem under a 'glasshouse' canopy, and its powerplant was one Junkers Jumo 211Da liquid-cooled Vee piston engine rated at 1,200hp. The type's dimensions included a span of 45ft 3.33in (13.80m) and length of 36ft 5in (11.10m), and its weights comprised an empty figure of 5,980lb (2,710 g) and a maximum take-off figure of 9,560lb (4340kg). The Ju 87B-1 had a maximum speed of 238mph (383km/h) at 13,410ft (4090 m), a climb to 6,560ft (2000 m) in 4 minutes 18 seconds, a service ceiling of 26,150ft (8,000m), and a range of 490 miles (790km). The inbuilt armament comprised two 0.312in (7.92mm) MG 17 fixed forward-firing machine guns in the wing leading edges and one 0.312in (7.9 mm) MG 15 trainable rearward-firing machine gun in the rear of the cockpit, and the disposable armament was 1,102lb (500kg), generally carried in the form of one 1,102lb SC-500 bomb on the underfuselage crutch that swung this weapon clear of the propeller before releasing it.

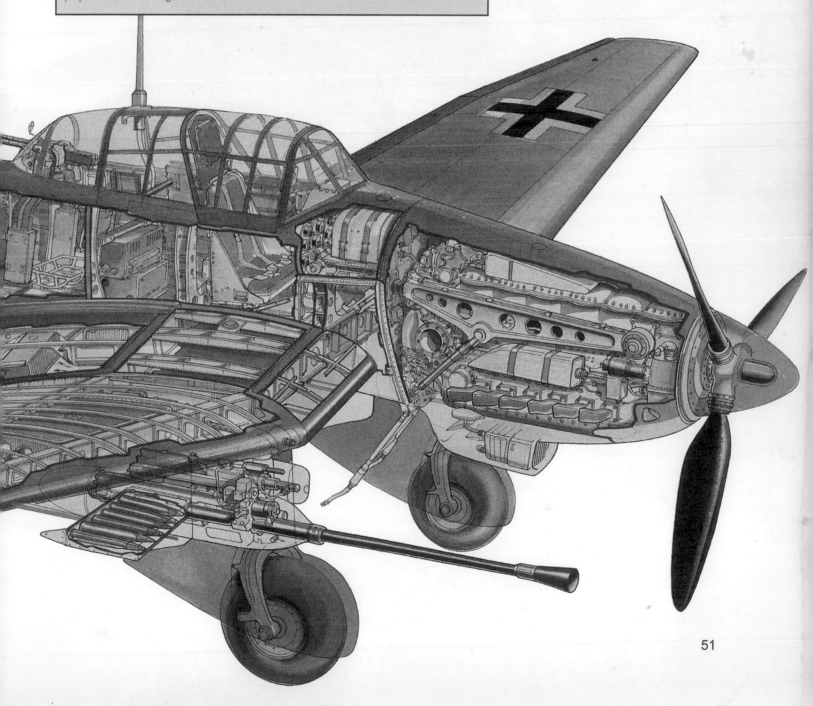

gull-winged fighter, single-engined P.23 Karás light bomber and twin-engined P.37 Lós medium bomber, all produced by PZL, the state aircraft company, and in the initial stages of the fighting inflicted some severe losses on their attackers. But the weight and experience of the Luftwaffe was bound to succeed in the end. After a few days the Poles could offer no large-scale aerial resistance, and the main weight of the Luftwaffe was switched to tactical support of the Panzer divisions, whose pincer movements were biting deep into Poland. German aircraft losses to ground fire were moderately heavy, but Luftwaffe aircraft continued to support the advancing Panzer formations.

If any doubts remained about the efficiency of the German armed forces, they were soon dispelled by the capture of Denmark and the most important strategic points in Norway by airborne and seaborne landings on 9 April 1940. The subsequent Luftwaffe operations in Norway followed the pattern set for them in Poland. The Norwegian air force was negligible, and the only major air support sent by the Allies was a number of British aircraft, most of them obsolete compared with the German opposition. It is interesting to note, however, that the Gloster Gladiator biplane fighter did achieve some success against the German bombers, although its use stood no chance of altering the course of the campaign, and this success is a useful reflection of the British pilots' high level of training and the relatively small qualitative

Above: With production exceeding 7,300 aircraft of all marks, the Heinkel He 111 was Germany's standard twin-engined medium bomber throughout World War II. The type was a useful warplane at the beginning of the war, but was forced to soldier on into obsolescence for lack of an adequate successor and, although the Germans achieved near miracles of upgrading the type and maintaining its operational capabilities, losses in the later stages of the war were inevitably high.

Right: The PZL P.37 Lós medium bomber was entering service at the beginning of World War II and was the best tactical warplane available to the Polish air force. Only a few aircraft had been delivered, however, and these were unable to change the course of the Polish campaign.

superiority of first-generation monoplane bombers over last-generation biplane fighters.

While the Germans were clearing up the last Allied pockets in central and northern Norway, momentous events were taking place in western Europe. On 10 May 1940, Hitler unleashed a huge offensive against the Netherlands, Belgium and France, which were defended by their own forces as well as by elements of the British services. The German attacks followed the Polish pattern, and were therefore centred on breakthrough and deep exploitation by the Panzer formations. These struck through the 'impassable' Ardennes to reach the Channel coast, splitting the Allied armies in two. The Germans then concentrated on eliminating the two halves in detail. With the Dutch, Belgians and French defeated to the north of the 'Panzer corridor', and the British and a number of their allies escaping from Dunkirk, the Germans turned their full weight upon the remnants of the French army holding that portion of France south of the corridor. The last elements of the French army surrendered towards the end of June.

Germany's next move was to attack the United Kingdom. Hitler had been amazed by the British declaration of war after the German invasion of Poland, and now urged the United Kingdom to make an honourable peace on the basis of the status quo. When this offer was refused, Hitler had no option but to plan the conquest of the United Kingdom, to be accomplished by an invasion codenamed Seelöwe (sealion). The German navy had suffered moderately heavy losses in the Norwegian campaign, and plans for the landings progressed only spasmodically. But Göring, promoted to the unique rank of Reichsmarschall for his part in the Luftwaffe's triumph over France, now declared that his air forces could render invasion unnecessary through the aerial destruction of the United Kingdom's ability and will to resist. This boastful claim led to the Battle of Britain, which was the world's first strategic all-air battle.

The Battle of Britain fell into three main phases: firstly, the attacks on convoys and coastal installations; secondly, the assault on Fighter Command's bases and fighter production centres; and thirdly, the campaign against urban areas. The coastal shipping phase began as France fell, and was typified by raids, usually by a few bombers with a heavy fighter escort, against British coastal convoys and the ports and naval installations on the English south and east coasts. With the aid of radar, the RAF was able to meet the Germans on equal terms and inflicted fairly heavy losses.

Since this coastal phase proved relatively ineffectual, the Luftwaffe high command decided at the beginning of August to attack British fighter bases and radar stations. The bombers would be used to lure the British fighters

aloft, and could also cause considerable damage to industrial areas and air bases, but again it was the fighters that were expected to inflict the main damage as the British fighters clawed for altitude on their bomber-interception missions.

This second phase of the battle exposed major flaws in the German air machine. The coastal phase had already proved the Stuka to be useless wherever the enemy had parity, let alone air superiority: the Ju 87 was hopelessly vulnerable at the bottom of its dive, where it lacked the energy for any kind of effective defensive manoeuvring. The fighter phase now revealed that the Bf 110, much favoured by the German propaganda machine and the Luftwaffe high command, was comparatively easy prey for the faster and nimbler British fighters. Losses were severe on both sides, but with the slower Hurricanes taking on the bombers and Bf 110s, and the Spitfires holding off the Bf 109s, the RAF slowly but inexorably gained ascendancy over the Luftwaffe, especially along the Channel coast.

On 7 September 1940, the Germans switched the focus of their offensive from Fighter Command to the great conurbations of London and the other great industrial cities of the United Kingdom. This change was demanded by Hitler, who was furious that Bomber Command had made air raids (as a result of navigational error) on Berlin. The German fighters were now ordered to abandon their roving (and therefore fuel-economical and tactically advantageous) loose escort of the bombers; instead they were to concentrate on close escort of the bombers. This denied the fighters advantageous use of their speed and agility, and also forced them into a

Above left: Conceived as an interceptor fighter to supplant the Hawker Hurricane, the Hawker Typhoon proved an abject failure in its planned role as its climb rate and high-altitude performance were inadequate, but then became one of the classic attack fighters of World War II. Operating at low level with its inbuilt armament of four 20mm Hispano cannon supplemented by two 500lb (227kg) bombs or eight unguided rockets each carrying a 60lb (27kg) warhead, the Typhoon Mk IB was one of the decisive weapons of the Normandy campaign in the summer of 1944, and wrought enormous destruction both on the German armoured forces as well as the logistical infrastructure on which the Germans were reliant for a sustained defence.

The Fairey Albacore was planned as successor to the legendary Fairey Swordfish in the carrierborne torpedo-bomber role, and offered such improvements as better performance and enclosed crew accommodation. Yet the type was never quite as 'right' as the Swordfish, which therefore remained not only in production but also in highly profitable service well after the Albacore had been phased out of first-line operation.

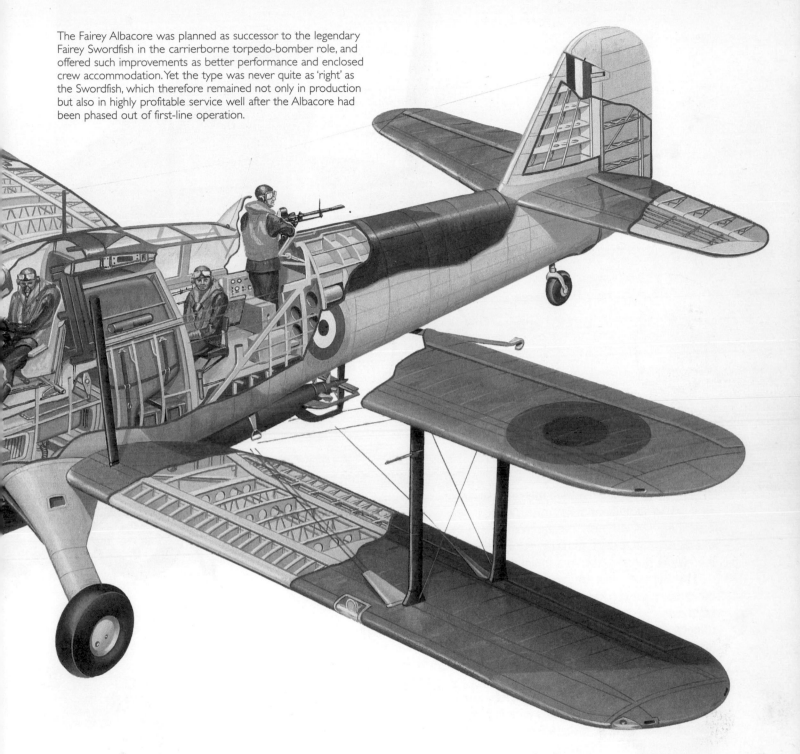

flight regime that was distinctly wasteful of their already strained range capabilities. In effect, the fighters had sufficient fuel for about 10 minutes of combat over London, after which time the bombers were left mostly unprotected, providing easier prey for the British fighters, which began to inflict increasingly heavy losses.

The Luftwaffe maintained its night attacks on British cities until the end of the spring of 1941, and RAF Bomber Command began a campaign of nocturnal raids on German cities. While the German bombers found it relatively easy to locate London and other major British cities from their

Seen here in the form of a Spitfire Mk I of No. 610 Squadron during 1940, the Supermarine Spitfire remains the most celebrated British fighter of all time. The type was already in full service on the outbreak of World War II, and was still in development at the end of the war in 1945, the intervening period of almost six years having seen a transformation of the type with double the horsepower (including a switch from the Rolls-Royce Merlin to the Rolls-Royce Griffon engine) for vastly improved performance, considerably increased fixed firepower now supplemented by a useful disposable load in the type's secondary fighter-bomber role, diversification into other roles such as photo-reconnaissance and carrierborne fighter, and a number of important aerodynamic enhancements.

bases in northern France and the Low Countries, British bombers found it far more difficult to find German cities. An operational research report at the end of 1940 showed that only a very small percentage of British bombs was falling anywhere near the intended targets. Yet this night bombing campaign was the only means available to the United Kingdom for direct attack on Germany, and the effort was therefore continued, gradually increasing in strength if not initially in accuracy.

The Blitz came to an eventual end in May 1941 for two reasons. Firstly, the twin-engined Bristol Beaufighter night-fighter, fitted with the new AI (airborne interception) radar, was taking an increasingly heavy toll of the raiders; secondly, German air formations were being transferred east for the invasion of the USSR. By June 1941 the United Kingdom was faced by only two fighter squadrons, but these managed to check British offensive operations over north-west Europe with the aid of the latest German fighter, the Focke-Wulf Fw 190. Powered by a closely cowled radial piston engine, this structurally sturdy fighter was highly manoeuvrable, carried very heavy armament, and enjoyed the advantage of performance generally superior to that of any British fighter.

The German plans for the conquest of the USSR were postponed for a short, but fatal, time by Hitler's decision to invade Yugoslavia and Greece in April. Belgrade was subjected to the now customary 'terror' bombing on 6 April 1941, the day on which the Germans crossed the borders. Despite the presence of British ground and air forces, the Germans swept all before them, although the Greeks and British managed to inflict relatively severe losses on the Luftwaffe. The Blitzkrieg combination of armoured and aerial power prevailed, and by the end of April both Greece and Yugoslavia were in German hands.

Supermarine Spitfire

BUILT to the extent of 20,351 aircraft, the Supermarine Spitfire was produced in larger numbers than any other British aircraft before or since, and served with the RAF and its reserve forces from 1938 to the mid-1950s. The type is seen here in the form of a Spitfire Mk IA, the variant that played so important a role in the Battle of Britain during the summer of 1940: the Spitfire was entrusted with the task of tackling the German fighters, thereby making it easier for less capable types (most notably the Hawker Hurricane) to destroy the bombers that were the main targets of the British defences. The Spitfire Mk IA was roughly comparable with the Messerschmitt Bf 109E in overall terms, but with a normally carbureted engine could not enter a negative-g manoeuvre and therefore had to half roll before diving, whereas the German fighter could bunt into a dive and therefore escape more readily.

Production of the Spitfire Mk IA totalled 1,583 aircraft with a powerplant of one Merlin III liquid-cooled Vee piston engine rated at 1,030 hp and an armament of eight 0.303 in (7.7mm) Browning fixed forward-firing machine guns in the wing leading edges. The Spitfire Mk IA's dimensions included a span of 36ft 10 in (11.22m) and length of 29ft 11 in (9.11m), its weights included an empty figure of 4,810lb (2,182kg) and a maximum take-off figure of 5,748lb (2,624kg), and its performance data comprised a maximum speed of 362mph (582km/h) at optimum altitude, an initial climb rate of 2,530ft (771m) per minute, a service ceiling of 31,900ft (9,725m), and a range of 395 miles (636km).

By mid-June 1941, most of Germany's offensive strength gathered along the Soviet frontier. Hitler planned to destroy the USSR as a political entity within four months, and a major tactical role was allocated to the Luftwaffe in the Germans' overall plan for the operation, codenamed 'Barbarossa'. The invasion began on 22 June, and from the first hours of the campaign the Germans secured total air superiority along the front. Tactical surprise was complete and most of the forward-based Soviet aircraft were destroyed on the ground, in the process constituting the majority of the thousands of Soviet aircraft knocked out or captured in the fighting's first few days.

By the type of paradox typical in war, this German success proved to be of enormous benefit to the Soviets in the longer term. Standards had declined radically during Stalin's purges of the Soviet armed forces during 1937 and 1938, and the Red air force was only just emerging from the shock of its mauling by the tiny Finnish air force in the 'Winter War'. In addition, at the time of the start of hostilities with Germany, the Red air force was saddled with vast numbers of obsolete aircraft that the government was unwilling to scrap. The Luftwaffe's action forced the communist leadership to accelerate the design, development and production of new aircraft.

The Soviets were already producing one of the war's finest ground-attack types, the single-engined Ilyushin Il-2 Shturmovik, and this was soon joined by the excellent twin-engined Petlyakov Pe-2 tactical medium bomber and the improving series of single-engined fighters designed by Lavochkin and Yakovlev. With just these four types at the core of their operational inventory between 1942 and 1945, the Soviets were able to produce vast numbers of aircraft that were austerely equipped by Western standards, but which were nonetheless ideally suited to the USSR's climatic extremes and

Left: The Hawker Hurricane was not as advanced a fighter as the Supermarine Spitfire, but was nonetheless a very worthy type that was available in larger numbers during the crucial Battle of Britain period, when it was responsible for the destruction of more German aircraft than all the other British defences combined. Of 'modern' aerodynamic design but with a somewhat dated structure, which did however ease production and repair, the Hurricane was obsolescent as a fighter by 1941 and was thereafter developed as a highly capable fighter-bomber for service mainly in North Africa and Burma.

Below: The Hawker Fury was one of the last British fighters to be developed in World War II, but appeared when the thrust of advanced fighter development was switching to turbojet-powered fighters. The type nevertheless entered limited production in its original landplane form and in somewhat larger numbers in its Sea Fury carrierborne form.

simple military tactics. Other types used were the Mikoyan-Gurevich fighter and the Ilyushin Il-4 bomber.

Although Germany's main interests from June 1941 lay in the east, the departure of most German air units did not lead to a halt of air operations in the west. Throughout 1941, fighter-bombers kept up a constant series of nuisance raids on targets in southern England, but the year was notable especially for the gradual emergence of the RAF as an offensive force, and for the increasing importance of air power in the Mediterranean theatre.

The most fascinating RAF aircraft to enter widespread service in 1941 was the de Havilland Mosquito which, with the possible exception of the Ju 88, may be judged to have been the war's most versatile aeroplane. It was almost certainly the most effective combat aeroplane of the war in terms of successes and achievements against losses. Conceived as a private venture, the Mosquito was planned as a high-speed bomber, using the same type of wooden sandwich-material structure pioneered in the pre-war Albatross airliner, and among the features demanded by the design team was a maximum speed so high that the Mosquito would need no defensive armament. Initially, the Air Ministry was sceptical, but when the prototype appeared in November 1940, its exquisite lines, extraordinary high speed and superb handling characteristics immediately revealed that the basic design was right.

Although the United Kingdom had accepted the philosophy of strategic bombing for some considerable time, the RAF entered World War II with no true heavy bomber. The Armstrong Whitworth Whitley had a useful maximum bomb load of 7,000lb (3,175kg) but possessed a range of only 470 miles (756km) with this load; the Handley Page Hampden could carry 4,000lb (1,814kg) of bombs for 1,200 miles (1,931km); and the Vickers Wellington Mk III had a range of 1,540 miles (2,478km) with 4,500lb (2,041kg) of bombs. These were all twin-engined machines, and the RAF

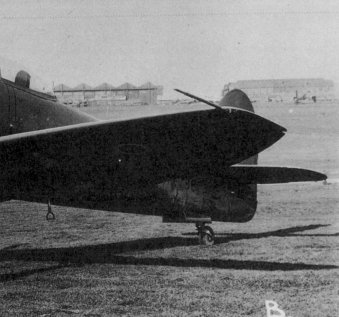

First Turbojet-Powered Fighters

THE world's first two turbojet-powered fighters entered service almost simultaneously in the summer of 1944, and were the British Gloster Meteor and the German Messerschmitt Me 262. The former was decidedly the inferior type in terms of short-term overall capability and long-term 'developability'.

The Meteor may be characterized as the piston-engined fighter merely translated into a turbojet-powered type by the replacement of the nose-mounted piston engine by a pair of bulky Rolls-Royce Welland (soon replaced by Rolls-Royce Derwent) centrifugal-flow turbojets in large wing-mounted nacelles, it had a fixed forward-firing armament of four 20mm Hispano cannon. The Me 262, on the other hand, had been more adventurously designed with cleaner lines, slightly swept flying surfaces, a powerplant of two slim Junkers Jumo 004 axial-flow turbojets in smaller nacelles attached to the undersurfaces of the wings, and a fixed forward-firing armament of four 30mm MK 108 cannon.

Development of the Me 262 ended with the conclusion of World War II while the Meteor remained in development and production into the mid-1950s, but this cannot disguise the fact that the Me 262 was basically the better fighter and, as such, the real precursor of later turbojet-powered fighters.

The Handley Page Hampden was a worthy but limited bomber designed in the mid-1930s as a heavy bomber, but was in fact a medium bomber by the standards prevailing at the beginning of World War II. The type carried an adequate bomb load of 4,000lb (1,814kg), but was poorly protected with a single 0.303in (7. mm) trainable machine gun in the nose and two 0.303in (7.7mm) trainable machines guns in the dorsal and ventral positions. None of these positions was a powered mounting for high rates of traverse and elevation, and the Hampden was further limited by the extreme narrowness of the fuselage, which made it impossible for the members of the crew to change position or replace the pilot if he was wounded or killed. Production totalled 1,532 aircraft including 100 examples of the Hereford with Napier Dagger engines in place of the standard pair of Bristol Pegasus radial engines.

The Vickers Wellington was extremely robust as a result of its fabric-covered geodetic (lattice-like) structure, and was the most successful British bomber of the first part of World War II. Although it carried only a slightly heavier bomb load than the Hampden, it had higher performance and was also better protected with two 0.303in (7.7mm) trainable machine guns in power-operated nose and tail turrets supplemented by single 0.303in machine-guns in the beam positions. As it became obsolescent as a bomber in the mid-war years, it was translated most effectively to other roles such as maritime patrol, transport and training.

Night Bombing

Aт the beginning of World War II, the British hoped to avoid the need for any bombing of targets on German soil but planned that any such attacks would be undertaken by day so that the bomber force could navigate more easily and attack with greater accuracy. Events soon dictated that bombing should be undertaken, but early experience revealed the hopeless vulnerability of British bombers to German fighter interception. The RAF therefore switched to night bombing.

The RAF had virtually no experience of long-range navigation by night, and no experience at all of undertaking such flying in formation. The result was a major decline in accuracy: although many crews reported in good faith that they had reached and bombed the target, subsequent reconnaissance revealed that only a very small percentage of the bomb load had in fact been delivered to the vicinity of the target, and virtually none at all on the target itself.

Growing experience and better training did result in an increase of navigational and bombing accuracies, but it remained impossible to strike at point targets such as particular shipyards or railway marshalling yards, and it became the British practice to bomb area targets, such as major industrial areas. The theory behind this system was that some of the bombs would almost certainly hit targets of direct military value, and that the rest of the bombs would hit and destroy the urban areas populated by the military targets' workforce, thereby reducing production as workers were killed, wounded, or merely had their sleep patterns destroyed by the need to take shelter, as they moved away from the area.

Throughout 1941 and 1942 the scale and effect of the British bombing increased as four-engined heavy bombers replaced the earlier twin-engined types and as navigational and bombing accuracies improved. These were never sufficient in themselves, however, and attacks of adequate accuracy could only result from the use of massive forces that might suffer very heavy losses. The right blend of force and accuracy was finally created by the establishment of the Path-Finder Force, which comprised highly skilled crews in aircraft often fitted with special navigational aids: these crews reached the target area shortly before the Main Force bombers, sought out the right target areas and then marked these with special pyrotechnic markers, providing a clear and unmistakable target for the Main Force bombers to attack.

The twin-engined Vickers Wellington has been overshadowed since the end of World War II by the four-engined heavy bombers that bore the bulk of the nocturnal raids on Germany from 1942, but was nevertheless of vital importance in the prosecution of the British bomber effort in the dark days of 1941 and 1942, and thereafter became just as important in a number of secondary roles.

had already accepted the fact that the combination of significant bomb load and useful range required the power and fuel capacity that could be offered only by four-engined aircraft.

By the autumn of 1941 no fewer than three four-engined heavy bombers had entered service with Bomber Command: the Short Stirling could carry 14,000lb (6,350kg) of bombs for 590 miles (949km), while the corresponding figures for the Handley Page Halifax were 5,800lb (2,631kg) carried over 1,860 miles (2,993km). Undoubtedly the finest of the trio, however, was the celebrated Avro Lancaster that could carry 14,000lb (6,350kg) of bombs over a range of 1,660 miles (2,671km), and also possessed a bomb bay large enough to carry considerably heavier special weapons over shorter ranges, for specific missions such as dam-busting, bridge destruction and the penetration of reinforced concrete U-boat pens. With the Halifax and Lancaster as its primary weapons, Bomber Command could begin to take the air war to Germany with increasing effect.

Throughout 1941, Bomber Command was learning the lessons of area bombing by night, and was building up its strength and skills for the heavy bombing campaign. Unlike the Americans, who were confident that their heavily armed daylight bombers could fight their way through the German defences, using their advanced Norden bombsights to succeed in pinpoint attacks on small targets of strategic importance, Bomber Command was convinced that night bombing was the only solution to anti-aircraft guns and fighter defences. The targets would have to be large industrial areas, in which bombing would damage industry and demoralise the civilian population, whilst keeping to a minimum the number of bombers lost to the German night-fighters.

The steadily improving capability of Bomber Command spurred a comparable development in the size and capability of the German night-fighter arm. Ground radar was developed to vector the Ju 88 and Bf 110 fighters into the correct area, and airborne interception sets installed in these night-fighters were used to locate the bombers at short range. British losses began to climb alarmingly during the early summer of 1941, but a counter to this trend was found in the form of 'Window'. This comprised specially-sized strips of metal foil, which were dropped in their millions to reflect the German radar beams and cause a totally confused picture of the situation on German radar screens.

The device was used with great success in 'Gomorrah', an operation that involved four Bomber Command raids in late July and early August 1943. 'Gomorrah' almost completely destroyed the great port of Hamburg. Thereafter, Bomber Command's growing fleet of heavy bombers turned its attention to the Battle of Berlin: a series of 16 great raids launched against the German capital in the winter of 1943 and spring of 1944.

During the summer of 1943, the heavy bombers of the US 8th Army Air Force began to complement the effort of Bomber Command in ever-increasing strength. Catapulted into World War II by the Japanese attack on Pearl Harbor on 7 December 1941, the United States had agreed with the United Kingdom that Germany was the prime enemy and should be destroyed first, and that only after this had been achieved would the full weight of the Allies be turned on the Japanese.

Most of 1942 was spent building up the US air forces in the United Kingdom, but from the summer onwards Boeing B-17 Flying Fortress and Consolidated B-24 Liberator heavy bombers started to undertake daylight

Undoubtedly the best and also the most widely remembered British heavy bomber of World War II, the Avro Lancaster was powered in most of its marks by four Rolls-Royce Merlin engines, was well defended, and could carry up to 18,000lb (8,165kg) of bombs or, in a special version, one 22,000lb (9,979kg) 'Grand Slam' bomb, the heaviest air-dropped weapon of World War II. This is a Lancaster B.Mk III, which was identical to the Lancaster B.Mk I except for its powerplant of four Merlin 22 or 24 engines, each rated at 1,640hp, made in the USA by Packard. The Lancaster B.Mk III accounted for 3,020 of the 7,378 Lancasters built, and its primary data included a crew of seven, a span of 102ft 0in (31.09m), length of 69ft 6in (21.18m), empty weight of 37,000lb (16,780kg), maximum take-off weight of 70,000lb (31,750kg), maximum level speed of 287mph (462km/h) at 11,500 ft (3,500m), climb to 20,000ft (6,095m) in 41 minutes 0 seconds, service ceiling of 24,500ft (7,465m), and range of 1,660 miles (2,675km) with a bomb load of 14,000lb (6,350kg). The type's defensive armament was eight 0.303in (7.7mm) Browning trainable machine guns located in three power-operated turrets: one in the nose with two guns, one in the dorsal position with two guns, and one in the tail with four guns.

probes into northern Europe. At first the US forces enjoyed some success. Then, in August 1943, the 8th Army Air Force launched its first raid deep into Germany. Warned by radar of the American build-up over the Channel, German fighters scrambled to attack the bomber formations, which were cruising at high altitude and producing highly visible 'vapour trails'. The German fighters picked up the American bombers while they were still a considerable distance from their target, and there followed a running battle to and from the target of Schweinfurt. The American bombers suffered crippling losses to the massed fighter attacks. A second attempt in October proved even more disastrous, and deep penetration raids were temporarily halted.

The problem lay in the fact that the bombers' defensive machine-guns lacked the weight and concentration to defeat the Germans' cannon-armed fighters. The bombers needed long-range escort fighters to protect them, but these were not available until the end of the year. At the time, the 8th Army Air Force's fighter squadrons were equipped only with the single-engined Republic P-47 Thunderbolt, a machine that was later to gain an enviable reputation as a heavy attack fighter, and with the twin-engined, twin-boom Lockheed P-38 Lightning that was too large and heavy to dogfight with the German single-engined machines. There was also an increasing number of North American P-51 Mustang fighters, but these were early American-engined variants that offered their best performance at low altitude, and were therefore unsuited to the high-altitude escort role. None of the American fighters had sufficient range to escort the heavy bombers deep into Europe, so they were confined to escort duty for the Martin B-26 Marauder and North American B-25 Mitchell medium bombers, creating havoc over the north of the continent.

One of the most important strategic uses of air power in World War II was the Japanese attack on the ships and base of the US Pacific Fleet at Pearl Harbor in the Hawaiian Islands in December 1941. The attack was a huge success in obvious tactical terms, for large numbers of American major warships were sunk or badly damaged, but in strategic terms it was a failure as it drew the USA into World War II and, by not finding the Americans' three carriers in the Pacific and failing to destroy Pearl Harbor's repair facilities and fuel supplies, could not deliver a knock-out blow.

Consolidated Liberator

BUILT in larger numbers than any other American warplane in history, a fact that is all the more remarkable as the type was a four-engined aeroplane planned for the long-range heavy bombing role, the Liberator was a truly excellent machine notable for its very long range (resulting from the use of well turbocharged engines to allow economical cruising flight at high altitude with the aid of its high-aspect-ratio wing) and the versatility that permitted its use in a number of basically related but operationally diverse roles.

In its baseline bomber version, the Liberator was the B-24 with a powerplant of four Pratt & Whitney R-1830 air-cooled radial engines each rated at 1,200hp. The first genuine production model of this series was the B-24D with a maximum bomb load of 8,800lb (3,992kg) and a defensive armament of 10 0.5in (12.7mm) Browning trainable machine guns installed as two hand-held weapon in the nose position, single hand-held weapon in the two beam positions, and two weapons in each of the power-operated dorsal, ventral and tail turrets. These 2,738 aircraft were followed by 791 examples of the B-24E with different propellers, 430 examples of the B-24G with a power-operated nose turret carrying two 0.5in (12.7mm) machine guns, 3,100 examples of the B-24H with an improved nose turret, 6,678 examples of the B-24J upgraded version of the B-24H with an improved autopilot, 1,250 examples of the B-24L version of the B-24J with two manually operated guns in the tail, and 2,593 examples of the B-24M revised version of the B-24J.

The maritime patrol version was the PB4Y-1 Liberator based on the B-24D and later bomber variants, and 977 if these aircraft were included in the totals listed above. An improved model was developed as the PB4Y-2 Privateer with the Liberator's twin endplate vertical surfaces replaced by a single, considerably taller vertical tail surface, and 736 of these aircraft were delivered for service after World War II.

The other main developments were the C-87 transport for the US Army Air Forces, the C-109 fuel transport for the USAAF in the Far East where fuel had to be lifted over the eastern Himalayas from India to China, the RY transport for the US Navy, the AT-22 flying classroom for the USAAF, and a number of Liberator variants for the RAF in the bomber, maritime reconnaissance and transport roles. Total production of the Liberator series was 18,482 aircraft excluding 782 examples of the PB4Y-2 Privateer and its few derivatives.

The Consolidated B-24 Liberator, seen here in the form of a B-24H, was used in virtually every American theatre of War, and is seen here in the form of a late-production aeroplane with a power-operated nose turret. Notable features were the high-aspect-ratio wing, tricycle landing gear with short nose unit to keep the fuselage as low to the ground as possible, good al-round defensive capability provided by the well-sited gun armament, and bomb carriage in two lower-fuselage weapon bay accessed not by conventional doors but by roller-blind doors that retracted out and then up round the lower fuselage.

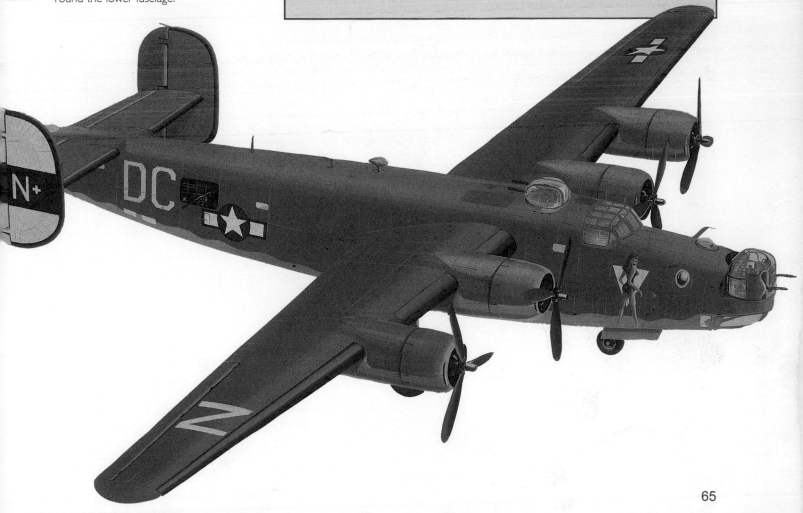

The British Spitfires and new Hawker Typhoons also undertook escort duties over Europe, but none of the Allied fighters had the range to penetrate the area where the main German fighter defences operated. Since the beginning of the combined bomber offensive, which had been launched on a highly organised co-operative basis by the 'Pointblank' directive issued by Prime Minister Winston Churchill and President Franklin D. Roosevelt in January 1943, the Germans had increased their fighter forces in Western Europe, and had taken a heavy toll of the Allied bombers.

The Mustang suffered an inauspicious entry into service, but was the fighter that ultimately provided the ideal answer to the Americans' escort problem. Designed to a British specification and produced in prototype form over a period of just 117 days, the Mustang was a departure from contemporary American practice in being powered by an inline, rather than a radial, piston engine. An Allison powerplant gave the new fighter excellent performance at low and medium altitudes, but the decision was taken to change to a British engine, the Rolls-Royce Merlin, and the Mustang became perhaps the best fighter of the war. Armed with six 0.5in (12.7mm) heavy machine-guns and able to use drop tanks (light external fuel tanks which could be dropped once their fuel had been exhausted, or on entering combat), the Mustang had excellent range and, once the drop tanks had been released, superb performance and the type of agility that allowed it to dogfight on equal terms with the best of the opposing German fighters. The Americans now had a fighter that could escort bombers as far as Berlin and back, and from December 1943 the 8th Army Air Force ranged deep into Europe with ever-increasing success. This success could be measured not only in the number of targets attacked and destroyed by the bombers, but also in the swelling total of German fighters despatched by the American escorts.

Joined from the beginning of 1944 by the 15th Army Air Force based in

The North American P-51 Mustang was the escort and multi-role fighter *par excellence* of World War II. Conceived to a British requirement and powered in its original versions by the Allison V-1710 liquid-cooled engine, the type was originally restricted by its indifferent altitude performance to the fighter-bomber and tactical reconnaissance fighter roles, but then the adoption of the Packard V-1650, which was the American-made version of the Rolls-Royce Merlin liquid-cooled engine, transformed the type's altitude performance while the addition of drop tanks allowed a considerable increase in range. The type reached its World War II mass-production apogee with the P-51D that introduced a cut-down rear fuselage to permit the adoption of a clear-view canopy providing improved fields of vision.

The North American P-51 Mustang offered a virtually ideal blend of performance, agility, firepower, viceless handling characteristics, and rugged strength to create a superb air combat fighter that could operate in the escort fighter and fighter-bomber roles. The definitive P-51D Mustang was powered by a Packard (Rolls-Royce) V-1650-7 Merlin engine rated at 1,510hp, and among its other data were a fixed forward-firing armament of six 0.5in (12.7mm) Browning machine guns, disposable armament of two 1,000lb (454kg) bombs or ten 5in (127mm) unguided air-to-surface rockets, span of 37ft 0in (11.28m), length of 32ft 3in (9,83m), empty weight of 7,125lb (3232kg), maximum take-off weight of 11,600lb (5,262kg), maximum speed of 437mph (703km/h) at 25,000ft (7,620m), service ceiling of 41,900ft (12,770m), and range of 2,080 miles (3,347km) with drop tanks.

Italy, the combined bomber offensive went from strength to strength, the Americans raiding by day and the British by night. German industrial potential was seriously affected, and the Luftwaffe's daylight losses were compounded by the increasing number of more expensive twin-engined and radar-equipped night-fighters destroyed by the British. The heavy losses suffered on the Eastern Front in the previous year, combined with the falling standard of pilot training, served to reduce the efficiency of the German fighter arm and ease the task of the Allied fighters.

In May and June 1944, the Allied heavy bombers turned their attention to isolating France from the rest of German-held territory, in preparation for the Allied invasion of Normandy. Canals were breached, spans were removed from bridges, railway lines and marshalling yards were turned into giant scrapyards, and all types of transport were harried unmercifully throughout north-western Europe. The German ground forces were virtually paralysed, and so heavy were the attacks on airfields that the remnants of the German air units in France were pulled back to Germany or southern France.

When the strategic bomber campaign resumed in July 1944, the British and Americans devoted their full attention to the German transport system and all types of power production, from electricity-generating stations to synthetic oil plants. Germany was virtually paralysed by the end of the year, with her armed forces desperately short of fuel. By the spring of 1945 the bombing campaign had brought Germany to the verge of collapse, and there were few worthwhile strategic targets remaining.

Meanwhile the Allies had evolved a tactical air power in most respects superior to anything the Germans had deployed between 1939 and 1941. The forcing ground for this Allied development had been North Africa, where a see-saw war had swayed across the continent from Egypt to Tunisia for some 30 months. The British had gradually evolved an effective and very flexible technique of close air support, based on the use of RAF controllers alongside the forward army troops to call in fighter-bombers and medium bombers as required from the 'cab-ranks' of such aircraft orbiting above the battlefield. By the end of 1942 the Allies had gained almost total air superiority over North Africa, and tactical air power played a decisive part in the final defeat of Axis forces on the ground by May 1943.

Although the tactical use of the fighter-bomber had been pioneered by the Germans over southern England, the real impetus for the development of tactically decisive fighter-bombers came from the British in the desert campaign. At first, obsolescent types such as early Hurricane fighters were fitted with makeshift bomb racks for use when the opportunity arose. There was soon a demand for

In its original and final forms, the Curtiss P-40 Warhawk series was powered by the Allison V-1710 liquid-cooled Vee piston engine, but in some of its most useful variants was engined with the Packard V-1650 version of the Rolls-Royce Merlin liquid-cooled Vee piston engine.

Known to the Americans and their allies by names such as Tomahawk, Kittyhawk and Warhawk, the Curtiss P-40 series of single-engined fighters resulted from a development programme in the later 1930s but was not a match in air combat for the best of European or Japanese-designed fighters. This meant the relegation of the P-40, seen here in the form of an aeroplane with Chinese markings, to the ground-attack role, and here the type's good low-level performance, steadiness as a weapons platform, load-carrying capability, and sturdiness were all assets that turned the P-40 from an indifferent fighter into a first-class ground-attack warplane.

aircraft that could carry bombs or unguided high-explosive rockets for use against ground targets, after which the aircraft could revert to its straight fighter role with cannon and machine-guns. A special Hurricane with twin 40mm anti-tank cannon was developed and proved to be a useful if limited weapon in the desert.

Most Allied fighters were eventually adapted to carry bombs and/or unguided rockets, with the Hawker Typhoon and the Hawker Tempest particularly effective in this capacity. Curtiss P-40 Tomahawk and Kittyhawk fighter conversions were important in North Africa and Italy, where the ground-support tactics in difficult terrain placed particular emphasis on flexibility and swift response. When the Allies invaded Italy in September 1943, the ground troops were often locked closely together, so the British and American fighter-bombers had to develop great accuracy in the delivery of their weapons. Although there were accidents, the overall standard of accuracy achieved by Allied fighter-bomber pilots was extremely high; and the system would be brought to its fullest development in the Normandy invasions of 1944.

From 1942, British torpedo bombers had been attacking German ships in European coastal waters, and from 1943 rockets and cannon, as well as bombs, were used on an increasing scale by Beaufighters and Mosquitoes,

Above: The Focke-Wulf Fw 200 Condor was designed in the period leading up to World War II as a transatlantic passenger transport, but was then pressed into more martial service as a long-range maritime reconnaissance bomber. As such, the Condor ranged deep into the Atlantic in the search for Allied convoys plying between the USA and the UK, vectoring in the U-boat 'wolf packs' or alternatively attacking ships with its modest but nonetheless useful bomb load. The Condor was also used as a launch platform for primitive anti-ship missiles.

severely restricting the movement of German coastal shipping and of Axis supply convoys operating between Italy and North Africa.

The main threat to the Allies at sea was the German U-boat fleet, and aircraft eventually helped suppress this threat. During the early stages of the war, anti-submarine operations were mainly undertaken by two aircraft: one was an obsolescent British machine, the Avro Anson, and the other an excellent American type, the Lockheed Hudson. But Hudsons were in short supply, and they lacked the range for long ocean patrols. Operations were therefore confined initially to coastal and offshore waters.

The requirement for four-engined aircraft offering the range for oceanic anti-submarine operations was appreciated at an early date. Bomber Command refused to relinquish sufficient numbers of land-based aircraft for conversion to this role, so Coastal Command's mainstay remained the reliable Short Sunderland flying boat. Gradually, however, Coastal Command acquired small numbers of Consolidated B-24s and Handley Page

The Consolidated PBY series, named Catalina by the British and almost universally known by that name today, was built in larger numbers than any other seaplane before or since, and was invaluable in the prosecution of the Allied war effort in most theatres. The type was originally developed and built as a pure flying boat, but in its PBY-5A form became an amphibian with retractable tricycle landing gear to enhance its operational versatility.

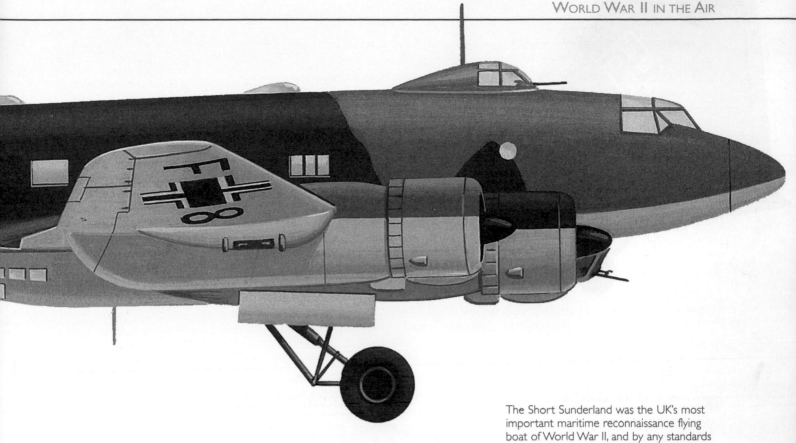

Halifaxes, which were soon operational over areas of the Atlantic Ocean where U-boats had previously been out of range of air attack.

With the new aircraft entering service, and with weapons effective against underwater targets, the 'Atlantic gap' between the limits of aircraft based in the United Kingdom and the United States was slowly narrowed. It was finally closed by naval aircraft operating from escort carriers, while the American Consolidated PBY Catalina flying boat was also used extensively. Gradually the Allied war against the U-boat became one of

The Short Sunderland was the UK's most important maritime reconnaissance flying boat of World War II, and by any standards was a classic 'boat of its type. It was extremely strong, possessed adequate speed and good range, and was well protected by multiple machine-gun turrets. When attacked by German fighters, whose pilots called the type the 'flying porcupine', the Sunderland generally descended to low altitude so that the German pilots could not attack its undefended lower portions, and then fought off the fighters with the guns in its power-operated turrets.

techniques with radar and weapons, and by 1944, aircraft and escort craft had combined to reduce the U-boat threat to manageable proportions.

Germany's main maritime aircraft was the Focke-Wulf Fw 200 Condor, a conversion of the pre-war airliner, which was used as a patrol bomber and a reconnaissance type. The Condor was adequate as a bomber, sinking large tonnages at times, but poor serviceability and structural weakness prevented it from becoming a major threat. The Condor made a first-class reconnaissance aeroplane, however, and had the Luftwaffe and German navy co-operated fully to exploit the type of information that could have been provided by the small Condor force, the U-boat successes would have been far greater, at least in 1941 and 1942. Other German aircraft that saw extensive use in the maritime role included two land based planes, the Heinkel He 111 and Junkers Ju 88 for torpedo and other attack modes, and flying boats of Blohm und Voss and Dornier manufacture.

By the end of World War II a revolutionary type of aeroplane had appeared. In the early years of the war, a considerable amount of work had been devoted to the jet engine, with the object of improving its power and reliability, and by 1943 both the British and Germans had experimental combat aircraft flying. Not only were they fast, but they allowed the designers to dispense with the large, vibrating piston engine in the nose of fighters, instead giving the pilot a much better field of vision and simplifying the task of installing a heavy battery of forward-firing cannon. Germany had advanced more rapidly than the United Kingdom, but official vacillation and Hitler's later insistence that jet aircraft be used as bombers had delayed the service debut of the world's first true jet-powered combat aircraft. Nevertheless, Germany had the Messerschmitt Me 262 twin-jet fighter and the Arado Ar 234 twin-jet bomber in service by 1944.

These were both greatly superior to Allied aircraft, but tactical misuse, shortages of fuel and of top-class pilots, and a variety of operational problems dictated that the few German jets produced could do little more

Right: The Mistel (mistletoe) was one of the expedients to which Germany was reduced during the closing stages of World War II in an effort to create a weapon decisive against point targets. The Mistel composite comprised two aircraft (in this instance a Focke-Wulf Fw 190 upper component and Junkers Ju 88 lower component) of which the lower carried a very large charge of explosive instead of the normal crew. The whole contraption was flown by the pilot in the smaller upper aeroplane, who controlled the flight and then, when within sight of a target such as a major bridge, locked the lower aeroplane on course and detached his fighter, leaving the explosive-laden bomber to crash onto the target.

Below: By the standards of carrierborne attack warplanes, the Douglas SBD Dauntless two-seat dive-bomber was relatively small and light, which made it quite nimble for a warplane of its class. Powered by a Wright R-1820-60 Cyclone air-cooled radial engine rated at 1,200hp, the definitive SBD-5 had a fixed forward-firing armament of two 0.5in (12.7mm) Browning machine guns, a defensive armament of two 0.3in (7.62mm) Browning machine guns in the rear of the 'glasshouse' cockpit, a disposable armament of one 500 or 1,000lb (227 or 454 kg) bomb carried on the centreline crutch and supplemented by two 100lb (45kg) bombs carried under the wing, or alternatively two 250lb (1,13kg) depth charges in its late-war role against submarines.

The Junkers Ju 88 was Germany's most versatile warplane of World War II, and rivals its British equivalent, the de Havilland Mosquito, for the honour of having been the most versatile warplane ever placed in production. The type was schemed as a high-speed medium bomber, but was then developed into other variants for roles as diverse as unmanned attack (see above), torpedo bombing, night-fighting, heavy attack and anti-tank work, and reconnaissance.

than show their manifest superiority, giving the Allies a disagreeable surprise before the end of the war. The only Allied jet fighter to see service was the Gloster Meteor, which was introduced in time to help defeat the V-1 flying bomb menace and take part in action over north-west Europe.

The Germans produced a fair number of experimental jet aircraft, along with the extraordinary Messerschmitt Me 163 Komet (comet) rocket-powered interceptor, and some of these types might have made a significant impact had the war continued. It was clear that German jet aircraft were aerodynamically superior to their Allied counterparts, and after the Allied victory there was a race between the Soviets, Americans and British to secure as much German research material as possible.

Before the jet engine reached a fully operational stage, however, several superb piston-engined fighters were developed as the last generation of such aircraft. These aircraft all possessed a maximum speed in the order of 475mph (765km/h): among the British offerings were the Supermarine Spiteful, Hawker Fury and de Havilland Hornet; American competitors included the Republic XP-47J Thunderbolt and North American P-82 Twin Mustang; and the primary German contender was the Focke-Wulf Ta 152.

Above: One of only three turbojet-powered aircraft to enter operational service in World War II, the Arado Ar 234 Blitz was a high-speed bomber, and was an excellent type that was virtually immune to Allied interception. As with a number of other advanced German weapons, however, it was a question of too little too late, andonly a few aircraft that were completed could be flown as Germany was desperately short of fuel.

Opposite top: Affectionately known as the 'Jug', abbreviated from Juggernaut, the Republic P-47 Thunderbolt was the largest and heaviest single-engined single-seat fighter to enter service in World War II, and found its *métier* as a devastating fighter-bomber with very good performance and a heavy disposable load.

Though none of these aircraft saw full-scale service in the war, some of them served as interim types pending the arrival of fully developed jet aircraft in the late 1940s.

The war against Japan also involved large-scale air warfare. Although the tactics used in the Pacific theatre were similar to those evolved in the European war, a number of differences were forced upon the combatants by the geographical circumstances of the campaign. The limitations of the aircraft, too, played an important part in both tactical and strategic developments. General Douglas MacArthur's reconquest of New Guinea, for example, took the particular form it did so that his land forces could enjoy all the benefits of superior air power, and the advances to the Marianas and Iwo Jima were largely dictated by the need for the former as a heavy bomber base, and for the latter as a base for escort fighters and as an emergency landing ground for bombers crippled over Japan.

Right: Without doubt the Messerschmitt Me 262 was aerodynamically the most advanced warplane to see service in World War II, and was in every respect a first-class fighter whose only limitation was the underdeveloped nature of its axial-flow engines, which were unreliable and also slow to spool up: this meant that piston-engined Allied fighters, most notably the Hawker Tempest and North American P-51 Mustang, could lurk near German airfields and then 'bounce' Me 262s as they came in to land.

Below: In the early part of World War II the Royal Navy discovered that its current two-seat carrierborne fighters were no match for single-seat landplane fighters, and an emergency programme led to the development of carrierborne versions of the RAF's two such fighters. The Hawker Hurricane was developed into the interim Sea Hurricane as the first step, and then came the Supermarine Seafire development of the higher-performance Spitfire. This was not ideally suited to carrierborne operations because of the narrow track of its outward-retracting main landing gear units and comparatively high landing speed, but the Seafire was nevertheless a capable fighter that at times proved very useful.

At an individual level, Japanese aircraft proved much more manoeuvrable than their Allied counterparts, especially in the first year of the war. Although a number of Japanese fighters had only machine-guns for armament, the redoubtable Mitsubishi A6M Reisen (Zero Fighter, nicknamed 'Zeke' by the Allies) also had cannon, enabling it to decimate the clumsier Allied fighters such as the US Navy's Brewster F2A Buffalo and Grumman F4F Wildcat, as well as the US Army's Bell P-39 Airacobra and Curtiss P-40, whose only defence lay in breaking off combat by means of a high-speed dive.

Gradually, the Allies introduced better fighters, and tactics were evolved to exploit the higher performance, superior firepower and better protection of these fighters to counter the superior agility of the Japanese machines.

The Grumman F4F Wildcat was the ablest fighter available to the US Navy in 1942 and the first two-thirds of 1943, and was largely responsible for turning the tide of the air war against the Japanese in the decisive period before and during the Battle of Midway in June 1942.

The Grumman TBF Avenger, also built in very large numbers by the Eastern Aircraft Division of General Motors as the TBM, was the US Navy's standard carrierborne torpedo and level bomber from mid-1942 to the end of World War II. Very sturdy, as were all the products of the Grumman 'Iron Works', the Avenger was so capable that little other than modest improvement in matters such as armament was required for the rest of the war, although a number of improved electronic features were added to enhance the type's operational versatility.

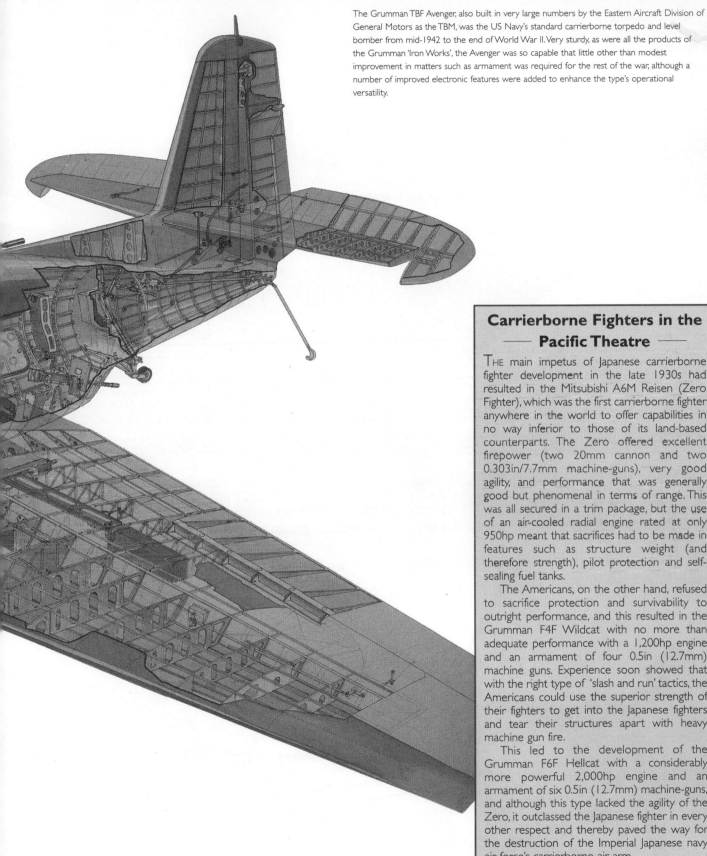

Carrierborne Fighters in the Pacific Theatre

THE main impetus of Japanese carrierborne fighter development in the late 1930s had resulted in the Mitsubishi A6M Reisen (Zero Fighter), which was the first carrierborne fighter anywhere in the world to offer capabilities in no way inferior to those of its land-based counterparts. The Zero offered excellent firepower (two 20mm cannon and two 0.303in/7.7mm machine-guns), very good agility, and performance that was generally good but phenomenal in terms of range. This was all secured in a trim package, but the use of an air-cooled radial engine rated at only 950hp meant that sacrifices had to be made in features such as structure weight (and therefore strength), pilot protection and self-sealing fuel tanks.

The Americans, on the other hand, refused to sacrifice protection and survivability to outright performance, and this resulted in the Grumman F4F Wildcat with no more than adequate performance with a 1,200hp engine and an armament of four 0.5in (12.7mm) machine guns. Experience soon showed that with the right type of 'slash and run' tactics, the Americans could use the superior strength of their fighters to get into the Japanese fighters and tear their structures apart with heavy machine gun fire.

This led to the development of the Grumman F6F Hellcat with a considerably more powerful 2,000hp engine and an armament of six 0.5in (12.7mm) machine-guns, and although this type lacked the agility of the Zero, it outclassed the Japanese fighter in every other respect and thereby paved the way for the destruction of the Imperial Japanese navy air force's carrierborne air arm.

The Martin B-26 Marauder was developed in parallel with the North American B-25 Mitchell to provide the US Army Air Forces with a high-performance medium bomber to operate mainly in the attack bomber role. The B-26 entered service before the Japanese attack on Pearl Harbor drew the USA into World War II in December 1941, and served with great distinction throughout the war. The type suffered a relatively severe accident rate in its early career because of its high wing loading and consequent high landing speed, but this problem was overcome by better training and the introduction of a wing of slightly greater area and incidence, and the Marauder then went on to become a highly effective warplane whose performance contributed signally to a record of very low operational losses.

Left: In the mid-1930s the Imperial Japanese navy air force led the world in the development of monoplanes for carrierborne deployment. Still convinced that success in combat would accrue from a combination of great agility and good performance, the service adopted the Mitsubishi A5M, later allocated the Allied reporting name 'Claude', as its first monoplane fighter. This could be fitted with a centreline drop tank for additional range (a pioneering development for the time) and had fixed landing gear with nicely faired main units, for the service decided that the additional weight and complexity of retractable main units would more than offset the possible slight gain in speed. The armament of two 0.303in (7.7mm) fixed forward-firing machine-guns was decidedly light, and an anachronistic feature was the open cockpit, which was demanded by pilots after the company had first developed the fighter with an enclosed cockpit.

Above: The North American P-82 Twin Mustang appeared very slightly too late for service in World War II, and was a successful attempt to create an escort fighter with even longer range than the classic P-51 Mustang. The Twin Mustang was in essence the fuselages and outer wing panels connected by a constant-chord wing centre section and tailplane.

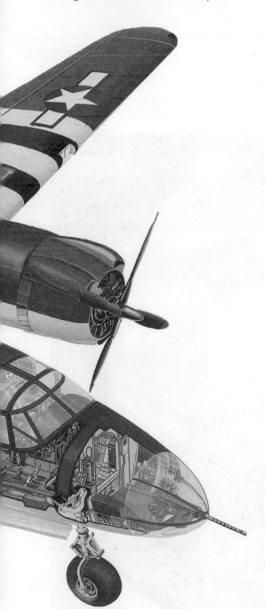

Martin B-26 Marauder

ALTHOUGH it saw service first in the Pacific theatre (initially with bombing attacks on Japanese-occupied New Britain from New Guinea, then as a torpedo bomber and level bomber in the Midway and Aleutian campaigns), the Marauder is best remembered for its part in the European campaign against the Germans. Here the B-26 was flown mainly by the 9th Army Air Force based in the UK and the 12th Army Air Force based in Italy, and was also operated by the British and, at a later date, French air forces.

Total production of the B-26 series was 4,708 aircraft including minor variants, and the first variant in this sequence was the B-26 of which 201 were built with the original wing spanning 65ft 0in (19.81m), a powerplant of two Pratt & Whitney R-2800-5 air-cooled radial engines each rated at 1,850hp, and a defensive armament of single 0.3in (7.62mm) Browning trainable machine guns in the manually operated nose and tail positions, and two 0.5in (12.7mm) Browning trainable machine guns in a power-operated dorsal turret. There followed 139 examples of the B-26A with increased weights, provision for a torpedo in place of the standard bomb load of 5,200lb (2,359kg), and a defensive armament of four 0.5in (12.7mm) machine guns. The B-26B, of which 1,883 were produced, introduced the uprated powerplant of two R-2800-41 engines each rated at 2,000 hp, revised armament including a package of four 0.5in (12.7mm) fixed forward-firing machine guns on the sides of the forward fuselage and, in the last 1,242 aircraft, a wing of increased span and area. The 1,235 examples of the B-26C were completed at a different factory to the basic B-26B standard, and the 300 examples of the B-26F were to an improved B-26C standard. The final major production model, of which 893 were delivered, was the B-26G development of the B-26F with equipment changes.

The B-26G may be taken as typical of late-production Marauder bombers, and its primary features included a crew of seven, a powerplant of two R-2800-43 engines each rated at 2,000hp, a disposable load of 4,000lb (1,814kg) carried in a lower-fuselage weapons bay, and a gun armament of eleven 0.5in (12.7m) Browning machine guns disposed as four fixed forward-firing weapons 'blistered' onto the sides of the forward fuselage, one trainable forward-firing weapon in the manually operated nose position, single manually operated laterally-firing weapons in the two beam positions, two trainable weapons in the power-operated dorsal turret, and two trainable rearward-firing weapons in the power-operated tail turret. Other details of this important warplane included a span of 71ft 0in (21.64m), length of 56ft 1in (17.09m), empty weight of 25,300lb (11,476kg), maximum take-off weight of 38,200lb (17328kg), maximum speed of 283mph (455km/h) at 5,000ft (1,525m), initial climb rate of 1,000ft (305m) per minute, service ceiling of 19,800ft (6,035m), and range of 1,100 miles (1,770 km).

The two most important fighters were the Grumman F6F Hellcat and Vought F4U Corsair, both high performance machines capable of carrying large offensive loads. The main strike aircraft were the Grumman TBF/TBM Avenger torpedo-bomber and Douglas SBD Dauntless dive-bomber later supplanted by the Curtiss SB2C Helldiver, all of which performed with great distinction.

The campaign against the Japanese in China was the responsibility of the Nationalist Chinese with support from the US Army, and Boeing B-29 Superfortress strategic heavy bombers began the strategic campaign against Japan from airfields in south-east China. From late 1944 they were joined by similar machines from bases on the islands of Saipan, Tinian and Guam in the recently captured Marianas group. The B-29s, carrying large bomb loads at high speed and over great distances, gradually eroded Japan's ability to fight, and caused severe civilian casualties with a series of devastating incendiary raids on the major Japanese cities.

It was the Pacific war, moreover, that finally proved the efficiency of strategic bombing. After the high-explosive and incendiary raids, two atomic bombs were dropped on Hiroshima and Nagasaki on 6 and 9 August 1945 respectively, and the terrible devastation caused by these weapons finally persuaded Japan that the war had to be ended without further delay.

A single aeroplane with just this devastating weapon could cripple a nation. For better or for worse, air power was supreme.

The symbol of the new era of warfare ushered in at the end of World War II was the mushroom cloud, which was the visible evidence of the ghastly destruction wrought at its base by the explosion of a nuclear weapon.

Conceived for the delivery of heavy bomb loads over considerable ranges by means of a high-altitude cruise, the Boeing B-29 Superfortress can be regarded as the first genuinely effective strategic bomber, for it was a warplane of this type that dropped the single atomic bombs on Hiroshima and Nagasaki during August 1945, finally to end World War II by forcefully persuading the Japanese that further resistance was pointless.

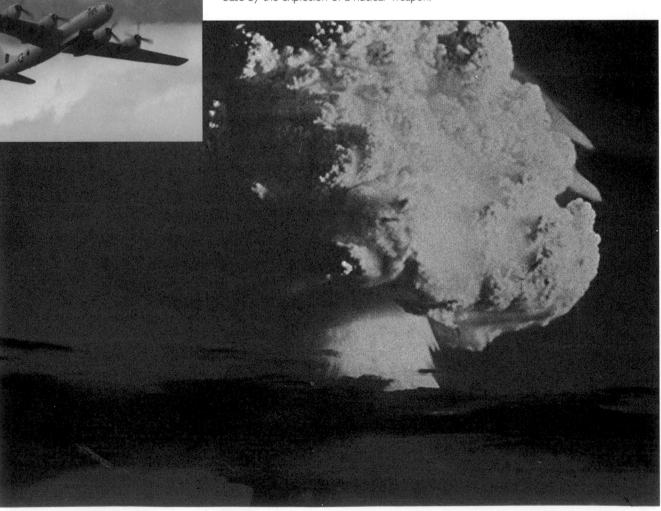

The Age of Turbine Propulsion

The de Havilland Vampire single-seat fighter was something of an oddity. Appearing just too late for service in World War II, it was an advanced type with propulsion by a single centrifugal-flow turbojet, but somewhat anachronistic in its early forms in retaining for its central nacelle the type of plywood/balsa/plywood sandwich construction typical of de Havilland aircraft from the late 1930s. Later models switched to an all-metal structure, and the light and nimble Vampire was at first a useful fighter, then a capable fighter-bomber, and finally an effective trainer in its variants with side-by-side accommodation in a wider nacelle.

D URING the closing stages of World War II, the major powers gained sufficient experience of turbojet propulsion both to appreciate its manifest advantages for military aircraft and to discover some of its attendant problems. Even in its original primitive state, the turbojet was designed, developed and produced in two basic forms: as the axial-flow turbojet and the centrifugal-flow turbojet. In the former, the air drawn through the inlet at the front of the engine is compressed longitudinally as it moves through a series of axial compressors on its way to the combustion chamber; in the latter, the indrawn air is compressed radially by a centrifugal compressor before being turned through a second right angle on its way to the combustion chambers arranged round the back of the engine casing.

The axial-flow turbojet was pioneered by the Germans, and the centrifugal-flow turbojet was the particular enthusiasm of the British. At first, the simple engine pioneered by Air Commodore Frank Whittle and built in prototype form by Power Turbojets was more than adequate in its core conceptual layout, and development of this core concept was entrusted to companies such as de Havilland, Metropolitan-Vickers, Rolls-Royce and Rover. From this process emerged the first two operational turbojets to power British

fighters, namely the de Havilland Goblin installed in the de Havilland Vampire, and the Rolls-Royce Welland used in the Gloster Meteor. Such centrifugal-flow turbojets were more than adequate for the performance limits imposed by the aerodynamic knowledge of the time, but late in the war the British began to appreciate some of the inherent disadvantages possessed by this engine layout, namely its considerable bulk (especially in diameter), and its need to turn the air flow through at least two right angles. Combined with thoughts of pushing forward towards high subsonic performance from the levels currently imposed by straight-wing aerodynamic theory, the disadvantages were sufficient to persuade British industry into the process of designing and developing axial-flow turbojets.

Perhaps a more urgent problem was that of fuel consumption. One of the

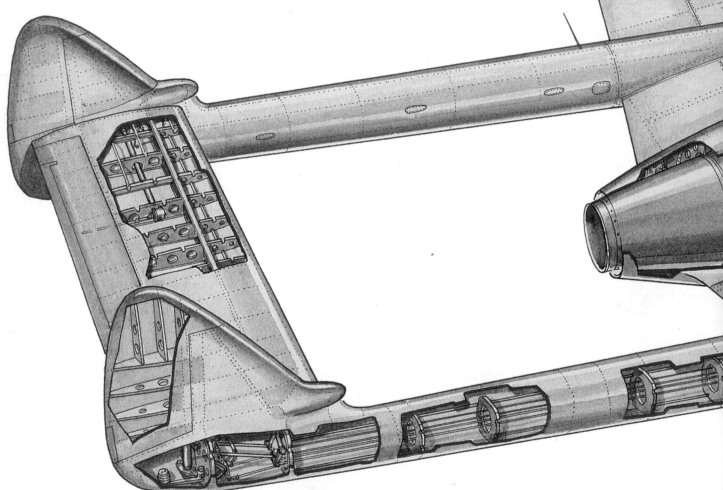

de Havilland Vampire

REMAINING in service into the 1980s in its trainer variants, the de Havilland Vampire was schemed as a pure fighter with single-seat accommodation and an inbuilt armament of four 20 mm Hispano fixed forward-firing cannon in the nose, was developed as a fighter-bomber with underwing racks for two 1,000lb (454kg) bombs or eight air-to-surface rockets each carrying a 60lb (27kg) warhead, and then revised with a wider central nacelle for the accommodation of two men in its trainer and then night-fighter models, the latter with airborne interception radar in the nose.

The Vampire FB.Mk 6 may be taken as typical of the fighter-bomber variants. It was powered by one de Havilland Goblin DGn.3 turbojet rated at 3,300lb st, spanned 38ft 0in (11.58m), was 39ft 9in (9.37m) long, possessed weights increasing from an empty figure of 7,200lb (3266kg) to a maximum take-off figure of 12,290lb (5,600kg), and was typified by performance including a maximum speed of 548mph (883km/h) at optimum altitude, initial climb rate of 4,800 ft (1,463m) per minute, service ceiling of 44,000ft (13,410m), and range of 1,400 miles (2,253km) with the two drop tanks that could be carried as an alternative to underwing weapons.

The rationale behind the de Havilland Vampire's configuration was the need to accommodate the bulky centrifugal-flow turbojet and to reduce thrust losses within the engine by using a jetpipe that was as short as possible. This suggested the incorporation of the engine in a short central nacelle, where it was aspirated via two wing-root inlets and exhausted immediately to the rear of the nacelle, and this in turn dictated that the tail unit should be carried on small-diameter booms extending rearward from the wing trailing edges and outboard of the exhaust plume.

turbojet's great advantages is its ability to operate on a fuel as simple as kerosene, but the early turbojet was so thirsty for fuel that the range of aircraft with such a powerplant was severely curtailed from that of piston-engined aircraft with the same fuel capacity. As a result, considerable effort was devoted to research designed to find a solution to the turbojet's high specific fuel consumption (the quantity of fuel burned to produce a given power for a given period).

Aerodynamicists were also discovering that, at high speeds, the air approaching and hitting the aeroplane's wings and fuselage was being compressed around the leading edges of the wings and other airflow entry areas. This compression resulted in considerable turbulence and drag, leading in turn to extreme buffeting that could cause structural failure. An early solution, applied in the North American P-51 Mustang and other piston-engined fighters, was the laminar-flow wing, which was much thinner in section than earlier types and was designed to smooth the flow of air round it, thus reducing both turbulence and drag. But even this solution could not alleviate the main problem, which was the high-pressure shock wave streaming back and out from the nose, the first part of the aeroplane to meet the airflow.

Despite their failure to co-ordinate research and apply its lessons effectively, the Germans had discovered the answer: sweeping the wings back out of the line of the shock wave. With a top speed of 870km/h (541mph), the Messerschmitt Me 262 twin-turbojet fighter that entered service in 1944 had modestly swept wings. This planform was adopted for structural and other aerodynamic reasons as much as for avoidance of the shock wave, but the success of this slight sweep, combined with the data revealed in captured German aerodynamic research, gave the Americans and Soviets an insight into the manner in which the effects of air compression could be overcome.

Even so, there was still much to be learned before aircraft would be capable of approaching the 'sound barrier'. Although there was an immediate reduction in the financial resources available for military hardware after the war, the lessons of the 1920s had been learned and a high

Designed in the closing stages of World War II for effective service from the second half of the 1940s, the Lockheed Neptune maritime patrol and anti-submarine warplane was a truly phenomenal machine that was originally designated as the P2V and from 1962 as the P-2. The type carried a substantial warload in the lower-fuselage weapons bay and under the wings, and in its original forms had powerful gun armament. The combination of two large piston engines and considerable fuel capacity provided moderately good performance together with great range and endurance, and in latter models two turbojets were added under the outer wing panels for boosted 'dash' performance. Finally, constant improvement and augmentation of the onboard electronics ensured that the Neptune was constantly a match for the warships and more particularly the submarines that were its main prey.

level of research was encouraged so that new military hardware could be developed quickly, should such a need materialise. The USSR and the United States took a quick lead in devoting a large proportion of their research effort to high-speed flight, and soon emerged with some formidable combat aircraft and impressive research types. Yet while they were absorbing German engine technology, most of the world's military powers used British turbojet engines, either imported or built under licence. The importance of the turbojet engine was well appreciated in the United Kingdom, and research and development continued as a high priority.

The Gloster Meteor had been the only Allied turbojet aircraft to serve operationally in World War II. After the war, the Meteor was quickly joined by the delightful Vampire, perhaps the last first-class fighting aeroplane of an unsophisticated type to enter service with any of the major powers. Although turbojet-powered, the Vampire in its initial form included a wooden central nacelle for the pilot, but had excellent handling characteristics despite the fact that its controls were unpowered. Good aircraft for their time, both the Meteor and the Vampire were considered more than adequate for their tasks by the government of a financially impoverished United Kingdom, and so no priority was afforded to research data that would be required for the creation of a more advanced type; the British government even opined that supersonic aircraft would be superfluous. This policy proved to be shortsighted.

The United States' main turbojet fighter of World War II had been the highly disappointing Bell P-59 Airacomet, which had not seen active service. Already on the drawing board, however, was the Lockheed P-80 (soon to be the F-80) Shooting Star, which would use a British-designed engine. Like the Meteor and Vampire, the Shooting Star did not feature a swept wing, but was clearly superior to the Meteor, which had established a world speed record of 975km/h (606mph) in 1946.

In 1947, North American, a firm that had been left behind in the race to build turbojet-powered fighters because of its commitment to the P-51 Mustang and P-82 Twin Mustang programmes, produced a classic fighter that succeeded largely because it incorporated the results of German research. This aeroplane was the F-86 Sabre, the West's first swept-wing fighter. The Sabre's lines were pleasing and, despite its lack of a suitably powerful engine, it was transonic (on or about the speed of sound) in a shallow dive. A year later the type was in service with the US Air Force (as the US Army Air Force was now known, having been made fully independent of the US Army). Export orders had been received, and several

First flown in the early 1960s and operational into the late 1980s, the Yakovlev Yak-28 was slightly supersonic and provided the USSR with a multi-role warplane type that was produced and operated in variants, identified by NATO as the 'Brewer' attack bomber with a glazed nose and capable of carrying a small nuclear weapon in its lower-fuselage weapons bay (most aircraft later being rebuilt for the electronic warfare and reconnaissance roles), the 'Firebar' interceptor with two medium-range and sometimes two short-range air-to-air missiles supported by airborne interception radar in a 'solid' nose, and the 'Maestro' two-seat advanced trainer.

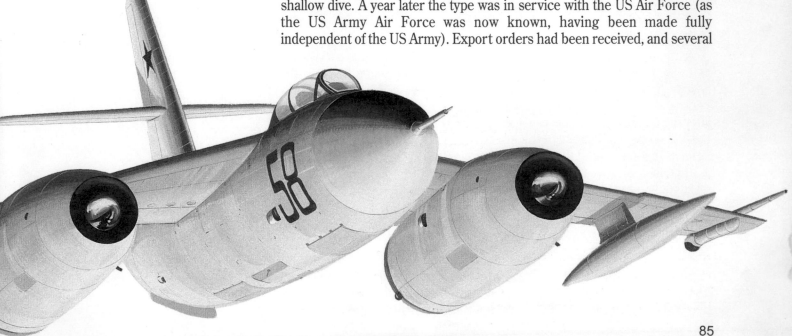

countries were interested in the possibilities of licensed production and development with different engines (the Orenda in Canada and the Rolls-Royce Avon in Australia), and different gun armament (two 30mm cannon in Australian aircraft replacing the standard American battery of six 0.5 in/12.7mm machine-guns). Far more advanced than other Western type, when introduced, 10,000 Sabre aircraft were eventually built.

Yet the Sabre had been preceded into the air by a Soviet type that would prove its greatest foe, the Mikoyan-Gurevich MiG-15, which first flew in July 1947, just three months before the Sabre. Although not as neat as the Sabre, the MiG-15 fully incorporated the results of German and Soviet research, and featured swept flying surfaces. Power was provided by a British-designed engine, for which the Labour government had granted export licences. Like most Soviet aircraft of the 1930s and 1940s, the MiG-15 was crude in finish and equipment, but was rugged, reliable and an excellent performer in the air.

Although the MiG-15 had entered widespread production and service use as early as 1948, later receiving the NATO reporting name 'Fagot', the Soviets had been more than normally secretive about their new fighter's performance. Thus, when American pilots first encountered the MiG-15 after the outbreak of the Korean War in 1950, they were completely startled. Indeed, it was the success of the MiG-15 against straight-winged American fighters that persuaded the US Air Force that the Sabre had to be deployed to this theatre. Even then, pilots soon discovered that the Sabre was marginally inferior to the MiG-15 in overall combat terms, but the combination of the American pilots' superior training and the Sabre's incorporation of a radar-aided gunsight enabled the American pilots to 'turn the tables' on their Soviet opponents.

By the early 1950s, the development costs of new aircraft had risen so sharply that governments and manufacturers alike were determined to wring every last particle of development potential out of basic designs. To the Western powers this usually meant the minimum of alteration to the

Designed and developed as successor to the classic Republic P-47 Thunderbolt heavy fighter from the later 1940s, the Republic F-84 fighter matured, like its predecessor, in the attack fighter rather than interceptor role, and many thousands of the type were delivered in the 1950s, not just as the mainstay of the US Air Force's tactical air arm but also as the core of the modern air forces being created by the European NATO countries against the threat of an aggressively minded Warsaw Pact alliance under the control of the USSR. The series was developed in three basic forms: as the Thunderjet fighter with a nose-aspirated engine and straight flying surfaces, as the Thunderstreak with a nose-aspirated engine and swept flying surfaces for higher subsonic performance, and as the Thunderstreak with inlets in the wing roots (leaving the nose free for reconnaissance equipment) and swept flying surfaces. The aeroplane illustrated here is an F-84F Thunderstreak, able to carry a small nuclear weapon.

basic airframe and engine, but constant updating of the avionics (aviation electronics), which are largely responsible for combat efficiency.

The first Western aeroplane of this type was the F-86D Sabre, which featured an advanced avionics package that provided an all-weather capability, and also enabled the fighter to engage targets automatically after the pilot had selected his objective. Once locked on to the target, the F-86D's radar and computer instructed the pilot as to course and speed until the target was in range: the computer/radar complex then extended the retractable rocket pack under the nose, fired the requisite weapons at the target, and retracted the pack.

Although some later American fighters (especially those of the US Navy) were fitted with a multiple cannon battery, from the Korean War until the late 1960s the Americans in general and the US Air Force in particular, preferred a primary armament of missiles. Initially these were unguided rockets rather than true guided missiles, and were fired at the target in salvoes in the case of the 2.75in (70mm) calibre Folding-Fin Air Rocket series, or individually in the case of the MB-1 Genie with its command-detonated nuclear warhead. Developed from the early 1950s, however, guided missiles with heat-seeking infra-red (IR) or radar guidance were in common service by the end of the decade. The radar-guided missiles fell into two basic categories depending on the specific nature of their guidance package: the active radar guidance system sends out its own search pulses and then homes on them, while the semi-active guidance system homes on the target, radar-illuminated by the attacking fighter, the guidance system steering the missile towards the source of the electromagnetic echoes it receives from the illuminated target.

Another improvement introduced on the F-86D was the use of afterburning, or 'reheat' as it is often called. In this system, extra fuel is injected into the exhaust gases of the engine, to mix and burn with the oxygen surviving in the exhaust gases, and so producing more thrust for little extra weight and complexity – but considerably increased fuel consumption. Such a system was commonplace on all high-performance military aircraft by the early 1960s.

The Republic F-84 Thunderjet was made superfluous as a fighter by the availability to the USA, and later to its allies, of the superlative North American F-86 Sabre fighters, exemplified here in action against a Mikoyan-Gurevich MiG-15 fighter, its primary foe in the Korean War. With a General Electric J47 axial-flow turbojet and swept flying surfaces, the Sabre was capable of high subsonic performance and was also a good dogfighter, especially in its later variants with a number of aerodynamic improvements. The type was also built in Canada with the Orenda turbojet for slightly improved performance, and in Australia with the Rolls-Royce Avon turbojet and the standard sextet of 0.5in (12.7mm) Browning machine-guns replaced by a pair of 30mm Aden cannon for better all-round performance and a much heavier air-to-air punch.

Even with afterburning and a fully developed engine, the Sabre was limited by its aerodynamic layout to transonic speeds. North American had recognised this factor, however, and had designed a Sabre-derived fighter that would be fully supersonic in level flight. Wings of markedly increased sweep and reduced thickness/chord ratio were added to a beautifully streamlined fuselage to create the Sabre 45 (the figure of the wing sweep angle), which was accepted for service as the F-100 Super Sabre. This was the first of the US Air Force's 'century' series of supersonic fighters, and introduced in 1954, at the start of a service career that lasted to the mid-1980s with some of the United States' allies.

Lockheed was also well aware of the limitations suffered by the current generation of fighters – for its F-80 Shooting Star and F-94 Starfire had received a rough handling from the MiG-15s in the Korean War, and the company now produced a thoroughly supersonic fighter. This was based on a design concept entirely different from that of the Super Sabre, however. Rather than use a high angle of sweep to reduce the problems of air compression, the Lockheed design team opted for an extraordinary layout that made its fighter resemble a missile, in that it was based on a large and basically cylindrical fuselage accommodating the pilot, electronics, a very powerful afterburning turbojet and most of the fuel. To this were added a large T-tail and a tiny but unswept wing that was tapered on its leading and trailing edges; thus the aeroplane relied on high engine thrust and its extremely thin wing to cut through the compression barrier. This F-104 Starfighter first flew in 1954 and was ordered into production for the US Air

A turbojet-powered warplane of the first-generation type, the Lockheed P-80 (later F-80) Shooting Star fighter was just too late for service in World War II, but was built in moderately large numbers in the late 1940s. The F-80 proved obsolete as a fighter in the Korean War, but was used with some success as a fighter-bomber and paved the way for the F-94 Starfire radar-equipped interceptor, and also for the T-33 trainer development that was built in considerably larger numbers and is still in widespread service during the mid-1990s for trainer and counter-insurgency roles.

Fighter Electronics

THE fighter emerged from World War II with the reflector or, gyro gunsight as its most advanced item of operational equipment. Developments in the later 1940s added the ranging radar to the gyro sight, and this helped to maintain the fighter as an excellent air combat platform. During this period, however, the bomber carrying nuclear weapons became an increasingly major threat, and although fighters could be vectored into an intercept position by ground radar, the control of collision-course interceptions gradually came to demand the adoption of lightweight interception and fire-control radar, the latter capability being required for accurate delivery of heavier gunfire or, more significantly, salvoes of air-to-air unguided rockets and the first generation of air-to-air missiles.

Throughout the 1950s the range, target-tracking and general capabilities of such equipment continued to improve to the point at which it became feasible for the Western nations to move away from the rigid implementation of ground-controlled interception techniques, in favour of a system that allowed the fighters to complete the interception on their own after being guided into the right general area.

A major breakthrough came with the development in the 1960s of miniaturised electronics in which thermionic valves were replaced by transistors to permit the creation of radar equipments that were considerably smaller and lighter, yet offered significantly improved reliability and overall capability. This permitted the development of radars that did not just search for targets, but also prioritising the tracked targets in order of probable threat, looking for targets below the fighter's flightpath in the ground 'clutter' that had previously made this impossible, and scanning the ground itself for navigation features and surface targets.

This process continued through the 1970s and 1980s, making the radar at once more capable and also less 'visible' to enemies so that the radar of today is a major element of the fighter's comprehensive sensor suite, which can also include infra-red and optronic systems for combination in the computer before presentation to the pilot on his head-up and head-down displays.

Force, which ultimately ordered only a small number of Starfighters, due to a change in its equipment policies.

The type was saved by a large order from the new West German air force for the F-104G, a much developed multi-role fighter, also ordered by several other European nations as well as by Canada, Japan, and a number of other American allies. The F-104G remained one of the most valuable combat aircraft used by the European countries of NATO until the mid-1980s, and is still in limited service with some American allies. It is also worth noting that Italy, in addition to participating on the European licensed production programme for the F-104G, developed its own variant as the Aeritalia (now Alenia) F-104S for service with the Italian and Turkish air forces.

The USSR had an avionics capability considerably inferior to that of the United States or even the European nations during the 1950s, and therefore concentrated its efforts on the full exploitation of current types. Thus there was a marked similarity between the MiG-15 and the MiG-17 'Fresco', which first flew in 1952. The structural problems and aerodynamic limitations which had caused the loss of many MiG-15s were overcome, and power was provided by a greatly uprated engine so that handling and performance were both improved considerably. Roughly contemporary with later models of the F-86, the MiG-17 had a higher performance than its rivals, but was not met in combat by its Western contemporaries. However, the MiG-17 was later passed to a number of Soviet allies and clients including North Vietnam and many Arab states. The North Vietnamese used the MiG-17 to good effect against the American 'century' series fighters in the early part of the Vietnam War during the mid- to late-1960s, capitalising on the Soviet fighters' agility and heavy firepower to close with their American opponents and engage in the type of turning fight that best suited the MiG-17's capabilities. The Arabs also used the MiG-17 in combat against French- and American-built fighters, although in this instance flown by the Israeli air force. In the Middle Eastern theatre the MiG-17 did not fare as well as in the Far Eastern theatre, for the Arab pilots were poorly trained and suffered heavily at the hands of the very able Israeli pilots. Thereupon, the Arab air force relegated the MiG-17 largely to the ground-attack role.

Just one year after the appearance of the MiG-17, however, the same design bureau produced its MiG-19 'Farmer'. This was the first Soviet fighter capable of supersonic performance in level flight, and in most respects it was a match for, if not actually superior to, the F-100. The MiG-19 had clear conceptual links with the MiG-17 and MiG-15, but was altogether a more refined design based on considerably improved aerodynamics, and a greatly improved powerplant comprising two Soviet-designed axial-flow turbojets in place of the earlier fighters' single British-type centrifugal-flow turbojet. The greater power and compact dimensions of the side-by-side engine installation allowed the design team to refine the somewhat tubby lines of the earlier types in preparation for supersonic flight. The USSR had also begun to catch up with advanced avionics, and the MiG-19 appeared in a number of models with different avionics packages for a variety of roles, including limited all-weather interception with radar and up to four primitive beam-riding air-to-air missiles.

Like the F-100, the MiG-19 enjoyed a long operational career, so it is right to say that both these Mach 1.3 fighters stood the test of prolonged service very well. The greatness of the MiG-19 can be measured in the fact that while the F-100 was soon switched from the pure fighter to the tactical fighter role, the Soviet fighter generally retained its pure fighter role. Even after it had been superseded in the USSR by more advanced fighters, the type remained a mainstay of the air forces of most Soviet allies, clients and satellites. By the mid-1960s, the West generally regarded the MiG-19 as obsolescent if not obsolete by comparison with the latest Western fighters offering Mach 2+ performance. Events in the Vietnam War and the Arab Israeli Wars of 1967 and 1973 then revealed the error of this judgement: its heavy cannon armament and light wing loading made the MiG-19 an excellent air-combat fighter at high subsonic speeds. This factor is still important in the mid-1990s, and the MiG-19 (including its Chinese-built Shenyang J-6 variants) remains in comparatively widespread service.

The pace of turbojet development was quite dramatic during the 1950s,

The Mikoyan-Gurevich was one of the most under-rated fighters of its day. The type was the USSR's first supersonic fighter, and as such the Soviet counterpart of the USA's North American F-100 Super Sabre. The Super Sabre later matured as a highly capable fighter-bomber and nuclear strike fighter, but the MiG-19 was generally retained in the air combat role. The type was a phenomenal achievement in aerodynamic and structural terms, for genuine supersonic performance was achieved with a powerplant of two small afterburning turbojets, and the long and very thin wing was remarkably stiff, allowing the incorporation of outboard ailerons (rather than the F-100's type of inboard ailerons) for rapid response in the rolling plane. Full appreciation of the MiG-19 and its Chinese-built J-6 variants came only in the late 1960s and early 1970s, when American pilots in Vietnam found that their highly supersonic fighters soon lost energy and thus manoeuvring capability in any sort of turning engagement, and thus became moderately easy prey for fighters such as the MiG-19 which could maintain high energy levels at high subsonic speeds.

Mikoyan-Gurevich MiG-19 series

ALTHOUGH it was a comparatively simple type, the Mikoyan-Gurevich can be used as an example of how the fighter was developed during the 1950s and 1960s. Vying with the North American F-100 Super Sabre for the historical niche as the world's first operational warplane capable of sustained supersonic performance in level flight, the MiG-19 resulted from a Soviet appreciation that the MiG-17, good as it was, was little more than a considerably improved MiG-15 and that truly supersonic flight performance could be provided only by a new design. Yet even when the MiG-19 had entered service, the Soviets pressed ahead with the development of Mach 2 fighters and thus undervalued the MiG-19. It was only later, with the advent of the Chinese version of this fighter, that the world came to realise the very real virtues of this high-performance fighter as a superb air-combat dogfighter, owing to its aerodynamic design and light wing loading.

The requirement for a supersonic fighter was issued in the autumn of 1949, and the Mikoyan-Gurevich design team soon decided that while the basic configuration of its earlier turbojet-powered fighters could be retained, albeit in much refined form, a new powerplant and a number of more advanced features were required. The Soviet centrifugal-flow turbojets derived from a British engine, the Rolls-Royce Nene, had too large a cross-section for sensible installation in a fuselage of the right fineness for supersonic flight, and had also reached the end of their useful development lives. The design team therefore decided to adopt an axial-flow turbojet of the afterburning type, together with flying surfaces with a leading-edge sweep of 58 degrees. As it previous MiG fighters, the wing was located in the mid-set position and was a truly remarkable structure of considerable area, high aspect ratio and low thickness/chord ratio, yet was immensely strong and also stiff enough in aero-elastic terms to allow the incorporation of outboard ailerons without any fear of aileron-reversal problems.

Work proceeded rapidly in the early 1950s, and as there were several engine options open to it, the design bureau designed its Aircraft SM in several prototype forms. The first of these to fly, in October 1952 was the I-350 with a powerplant of one Lyul'ka AL-5 or AL-5F turbojet. The I-360 second prototype flew toward the end of the year with a radically different powerplant of two small Mikulin AM-5 (later called Tumanskii RD-5) turbojets arranged side-by-side in the rear fuselage. The I-370 third prototype, which also flew in 1952, was powered by two Klimov VK-7F turbojets. It is thought that the first and second prototypes had the same pattern of tail unit as the MiG-15 and MiG-17, with the horizontal surface located part-way up the vertical tail surface, but that the third prototype may have introduced the type of tail unit adopted for the production model, with the tailplane lowered from the vertical surface to the upper part of the rear fuselage.

Trials revealed the superiority of the I-360's powerplant, and this was adopted for the pre-production model, which was authorised in 1953 with the designation MiG-19F and subsequent NATO reporting designation of 'Farmer-A'. The first of these aircraft flew during September 1953, and the type was delivered for service evaluation from December with a powerplant of two AM-5F turbojets each rated at 6,702lb st (29.81kN) with afterburning.

Later redesignated MiG-19SF, the MiG-19S 'Farmer-C' was the first major production version, and was developed under great pressure to overcome the longitudinal control problem encountered at transonic speed by the first two variants, which used a fixed tailplane and separate elevators. The MiG-19S introduced an all-moving slab tailplane with anti-flutter masses ahead of the leading edge. This effectively cured the longitudinal control problem, and other changes introduced with the MiG-19S were a powerplant of two redesignated RD-9B (later improved RD-9BF) turbojets, spoilers for improved roll control, an additional air brake in the ventral position, a revised control system, and a gun armament of three long-barrel 30mm cannon in place of the mixed battery of 23 and 37mm weapons carried by the earlier aircraft.

The MiG-19PM 'Farmer-D' was the limited all-weather development of the MiG-19SF with the cannon armament deleted and four underwing hardpoints added for a quartet of RS-2 or K-5 (AA-1 'Alkali') air-to-air missiles (AAMs) employed in conjunction with the 'Scan Odd' radar used for target acquisition and guidance of the beam-riding AAMs. The type was also produced in China as the Shenyang J-6, and the variants of this series included the J-6 'Farmer' version of the MiG-19SF 'Farmer-C', produced after the signature of a licence agreement in January 1958. Deliveries began in December 1961 of the J-6 in its initial form with an armament of three 30mm cannon. Since that time the type has been built in large numbers and also exported with the designation F-6, impressing customers with the excellence of the finish and the great attention paid to detail during the design and manufacturing processes.

The J-6A 'Farmer' is the Chinese equivalent of the MiG-19PF with a fixed armament of two 30mm cannon (in the wing roots) and radar to provide limited all-weather interception capability. The type was exported as the F-6A. The J-6B 'Farmer' is the Chinese equivalent of the MiG-19PM 'Farmer-D' with the two 30 mm cannon supplemented by two PL-1 semi-active radar-homing AAMs derived from the Soviet RS-2 or K-5 (AA-1 'Alkali') and used in association with interception radar. The J-6C 'Farmer' is a development for the day-fighter role with the brake chute relocated to a bullet fairing at the base of the rudder. The J-6Xin 'Farmer' is a development of the J-6A with Chinese radar in a sharp-tipped radome on the splitter plate rather than Soviet radar in the inlet centrebody.

Built by Tianjin rather than Shenyang, the JJ-6 'Farmer' is a trainer, development equivalent to (but not identical with) the MiG-19UTI that was developed in prototype form in the USSR but not placed in production. The JJ-6 has its forward fuselage lengthened forward of the wing to provide volume for the insertion of a tandem-seat cockpit.

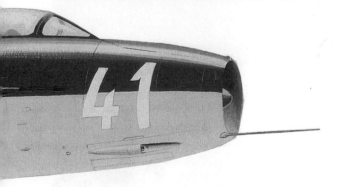

however, and the F-104, which appeared only a year after the MiG-19, was far superior in terms of legend performance, with a maximum level speed in excess of Mach 2 and a far superior climb rate and service ceiling.

In the early 1950s, Republic also produced a supersonic fighter, developing the F-84F Thunderstreak from the F-84 Thunderjet, the substitution of swept wings for straight flying surfaces on a fuselage that was otherwise little modified affording a useful increase in overall performance. This produced an improved fighter at minimal cost, but the Thunderstreak was only an interim type, despite a long and distinguished career as a fighter-bomber and reconnaissance aeroplane with the US Air Force and several allied nations.

To create a truly supersonic type, the Republic design team echoed the North American team in the adoption of highly swept flying surfaces, a sleek fuselage and a powerful turbojet with full afterburning. First flown in 1955, this Republic aeroplane was the F-105 Thunderchief, one of the classic US Air Force aircraft of the period after World War II. Although it was classified as a fighter, the Thunderchief was in reality a massive and hard-hitting strike and attack aeroplane, characterised not only by its high supersonic performance but also by its incorporation of an internal weapon bay to supplement the hardpoints that had become standard for the carriage of external drop loads. Nicknamed 'Thud', the Thunderchief also featured an advanced avionics suite that created a number of maintenance problems but found a new lease of life in the 1960s during the Vietnam War. Even though many analysts had decided that the nuclear-capable F-105 was obsolescent, the type was revealed by operations to be versatile and capable of absorbing the levels of battle damage that would have downed most other types. Even

The Republic F-105 Thunderchief was conceived as a highly capable supersonic strike warplane able to deliver nuclear weapons in the operational and tactical roles. After a number of difficult teething problems caused by its very advanced nature, the type was used in the conventional attack role during the Vietnam War and proved highly successful. The Thunderchief could also be refuelled in the air by the US Air Force's standard system of the type, namely the flying boom carried by the Boeing KC-135 Stratotanker: this boom was 'flown' into a receptacle on the receiver warplane by an operator in the tanker, and fuel was passed down the boom after a positive lock had been achieved between the boom and the receiver warplane.

The two-seat trainer model of the Thunderchief was also pressed into active service after conversion to the 'Wild Weasel' configuration with additional electronics for the detection and localisation of enemy air-defence radars that could then be destroyed by the high-explosive/fragmentation bombs or specialist anti-radar missiles (typically the AGM-45 Shrike or AGM-78 Standard ARM) carried by the Thunderchief, or alternatively by the weapons carried by accompanying warplanes supplied with the required targeting information by radio or data-link.

when damaged on the way to the target, the F-105 could often deliver its weapons load (now generally carried on one under-fuselage and four under-wing hardpoints) with pinpoint accuracy and only then turn for home.

With their powerful engines and advanced aerodynamic features, multi-role fighters could, by the late 1950s, carry an offensive load far greater than could be stowed inside the airframe, even if it had been possible to locate a weapons bay among the masses of avionics equipment accommodated throughout the fuselage. Pioneered during World War II, streamlined pylons under the wings and fuselage could accept a dazzling variety of under-wing stores. Not only bombs, but unguided rockets either singly if they were of large calibre or in multiple launcher pods if they were of small calibre, guided missiles of the air-to-air and/or air-to-surface varieties, napalm tanks, chemical tanks, drop tanks for extra fuel, and other offensive stores could be carried. The mass of wiring and plumbing needed to connect the stores and tanks to onboard computers and the aeroplane's main fuel system greatly increased the complexity of the problems faced by the large design teams.

Meanwhile, the Europeans were advancing more slowly than the Americans and the Soviets. World War II, had devastated Europe, and of the major aeronautical powers before World War II, only the United Kingdom and France were in any position to design and construct advanced combat aircraft. Yet the British government could foresee no war before the late 1950s and, with finance in short supply, the development of new fighting aircraft received a low priority. In France the work of reconstruction after World War II was more urgent and, despite a number of interesting experiments, the combat aircraft brought into service were chosen for their serviceability rather than for inspirational design or high performance.

The limitations of the United Kingdom's Meteor and Vampire as front-line fighters were highlighted by the Korean War, but the lack of research and development in the previous years had left the British aircraft industry in no position to advance the production of a new fighter. In 1952, the United Kingdom was placed in the humiliating position of having to accept 430 Sabres built by Canadair and paid for by the American and Canadian governments. Two years later, however, as several supersonic types were being introduced in the USSR and the United States, two swept-wing but only transonic British fighters entered service after prolonged development.

The first of these was the Supermarine Swift, whose production programme was curtailed as a result of the type's intransigent aerodynamic

problems; the second was the classic Hawker Hunter, perhaps the best transonic fighter and ground-support aircraft of its kind. With clean lines, excellent handling characteristics and a good load-carrying capacity, the Hunter was built in greater numbers than any other post-war British aeroplane, and is still in first-line service with several smaller air forces during the mid-1990s.

French fighter aircraft have been supplied almost exclusively by the firm set up in 1945 by Marcel Bloch, whose aircraft manufacturing company had been nationalised in 1937 as part of the SNCASO group. Returning from Germany, where he had been incarcerated during the war, he changed his surname to Dassault (his codename in the wartime resistance), and built up the company bearing his new name into the biggest military aircraft manufacturer in France. The machines supplied by Dassault have been based on sound engineering and inspired design, with costs carefully kept down by repeating as many components and ideas as possible from design to design.

Below left: The most successful European-built fighter in numerical as well as operational terms, the Dassault Mirage III resulted from a requirement for a lightweight interceptor but matured as a medium-weight interceptor that was soon rendered superfluous in its designed fast-climbing role by the disappearance of the high-altitude bomber after the introduction of effective surface-to-air missile systems. The type's development then centred on the creation of the Mirage IIIE multi-role fighter and Mirage IIIR reconnaissance variants.

Opposite: The English Electric Lightning was initially conceived as a supersonic research type but later developed as an interceptor and finally as a fighter-bomber. The most notable features of the Lightning were its angular flying surfaces and the use of a twin-engined powerplant in which the engines were superimposed to avoid the possibility of asymmetric control problems in the event of one engine failing. Both engines were aspirated via a circular nose inlet whose centrebody contained the antenna for the airborne interception radar. The Lightning was very fast and possessed a superb rate of climb but, in common with most other British-designed fighters, was notably short of range on internal fuel and was only lightly armed with a mere two short-range air-to-air missiles on the sides of the forward fuselage. Both these limitations were addressed in later models, which introduced a large ventral installation in which the forward part carried two 30mm Aden fixed forward-firing cannon and the rear part extra fuel. The last models for export, to Kuwait and Saudi Arabia, had underwing and overwing hardpoints for the carriage of missiles and/or bombs.

The first turbojet-powered Dassault fighter was the Ouragan (hurricane), which was built in moderate numbers for the French and Indian air forces before being replaced by the more advanced swept-wing Mystère. The Mystère was built in some numbers, both for the home market and for export, and was the first French aircraft to exceed the speed of sound, although only in a shallow dive. Just as the F-100 had been evolved in concept terms from the F-86, the Super Mystère, of which Dassault flew in prototype form in 1955, was the truly supersonic development of the Mystère. With its more streamlined fuselage, a Rolls-Royce Avon axial-flow afterburning turbojet and very thin wings, it proved a first-class fighter, and served the Israeli air force well in combat.

The first Mach 2 European fighter was the English Electric (later British Aircraft Corporation and finally British Aerospace) Lightning. This had entered service in 1960, after a 13-year design and development period that had turned a supersonic research aeroplane into a phenomenal fast-climbing interceptor whose two main limitations were indifferent armament and poor range.

The Dassault Mirage III, adopted in 1961, appeared six years after the first flight of the Mirage I lightweight prototype. The prolonged gestation periods of these fighters, comparing poorly with the speed at which the Soviets and Americans were able to put new types into service, was a clear indication of weakness in the European aeronautical industry and the strength of the superpowers.

The Mirage III has been the most successful European combat aeroplane designed since World War II, and has formed the basis of a large number of advanced and high-performance combat aircraft. Essentially a scaled-up Mirage III, the Mirage IV is a Mach 2 bomber for the delivery of France's atomic bombs.

The Mirage 5 was designed to an Israeli requirement as a simplified clear-weather version of the all-weather Mirage III for use as a ground-attack fighter, but since upgraded in most cases to Mirage III standards or higher as miniaturised electronics were developed.

The most successful exponent of the Dassault Mirage III series in operational terms has been the Israeli Defence Force/Air Force, which used its aircraft to devastating effect in the first hours of the 1967 'Six-Day War'. Knowing that Egypt, Jordan and Syria were planning to launch a combined offensive to crush it, Israel planned and executed a militarily decisive pre-emptive campaign that resulted in the capture of the Sinai from Egypt, eastern Jerusalem and the 'East Bank' of the Jordan river from Jordan, and much of the Golan Heights from Syria. The key to this extraordinary success was Israel's incredible series of preliminary air raids, which caught most of the Arab air power on the ground and destroyed at least three-quarters of it for virtually no Israeli losses. The most advanced type used in these raids was the Mirage III, which provided air cover as well as delivering crushing attacks on surface targets.

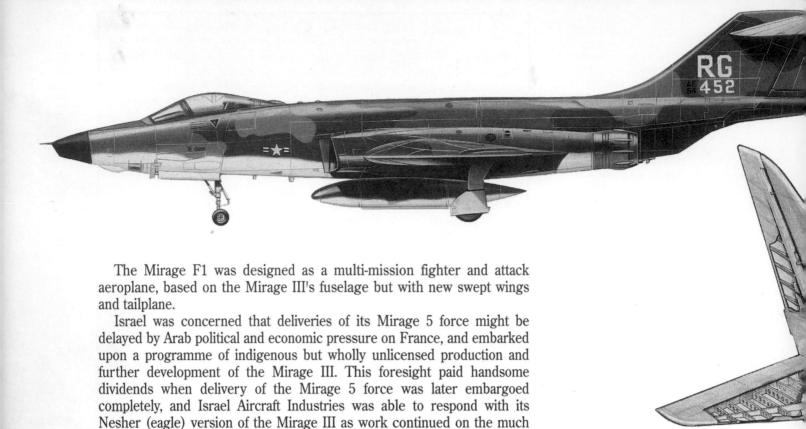

The Mirage F1 was designed as a multi-mission fighter and attack aeroplane, based on the Mirage III's fuselage but with new swept wings and tailplane.

Israel was concerned that deliveries of its Mirage 5 force might be delayed by Arab political and economic pressure on France, and embarked upon a programme of indigenous but wholly unlicensed production and further development of the Mirage III. This foresight paid handsome dividends when delivery of the Mirage 5 force was later embargoed completely, and Israel Aircraft Industries was able to respond with its Nesher (eagle) version of the Mirage III as work continued on the much upgraded Kfir (lion cub) derivative with an American turbojet and an advanced suite of Israeli electronics. Israel used its Mirage IIIs to stunning effect in the 1967 'Six-Day War' and had introduced the Nesher in time for the 'Yom Kippur' War of 1973.

Surplus Neshers were later exported to Argentina with the name Dagger, and were used against the British during the Falklands campaign. In Israel, further development of the Kfir produced the Kfir-C2, with canard foreplanes to improve field performance and to enhance manoeuvrability in air combat, and Israel has continued to develop this useful type in variants with more refined aerodynamics, greater power from a 'tweaked' engine and, most importantly of all, increasingly sophisticated electronics in single- and two-seat variants.

Many exported Mirage IIIs and Mirage 5s have been upgraded to a comparable standard, and South Africa undertook a comparable upgrade effort to produce the Atlas Cheetah, by rebuilding French aircraft delivered before the imposition of a United Nations' embargo of arms supplies as a supposed counter to South Africa's policy of separate racial development. This embargo was lifted in 1994 after the swearing-in of a new multi-racial South African government, and this has opened the possibility of South African exports or involvement in further Mirage III/5 upgrades.

The basic design of the remarkable Mirage III has proved enormously adaptable and, with different engines, flying surfaces, avionics and armament can undertake a variety of combat tasks ranging from short-range interception to medium-range operational-level nuclear strike bombing, all-weather fighting, training, daylight ground attack and reconnaissance. The Mirage III and Mirage 5 are still operational in some numbers with European air forces although they are now rapidly declining in importance as more advanced types have assumed primary roles, but they are likely to remain among the most valuable combat types of several South American and African countries for many years. Indeed,

Opposite: The McDonnell F-101 Voodoo was planned as a fighter that could escort American strategic bombers as they penetrated Soviet air space, but range of the required order was impossible with the turbojet engines of the period, and the F-101 was therefore developed initially as a day interceptor, then as an all-weather interceptor, and finally as a reconnaissance aeroplane. In this last capacity the RF-101 was extensively used in the dangerous days of the Cuban Missile Crisis of 1962, and was one of the key elements that allowed the USA to determine the extent and nature of the Soviet involvement in Cuba.

McDonnell Douglas A-4 Skyhawk

ONE of the most remarkable warplanes of all time, the Skyhawk was designed by Douglas, before its merger with McDonnell, as the A4D carrierborne light-attack bomber which first flew in June 1954 but then matured during the 1960s as the A-4 multi-role land-based as well as carrierborne warplane. The design team's objective was to produce the smallest, lightest and therefore cheapest type that could fulfil the complete mission expected of it, and so successful was the result that the prototype turned the scales at a maximum weight only half that fixed by the US Navy as its upper limit, yet it was capable of high subsonic speed and, in unladen form, fighter-like agility.

As might be expected of so important a type, the Skyhawk went through a number of forms with steadily increasing capabilities (in terms of weapons load and electronics, the latter accommodated in an enlarged 'hump' fairing to the rear of the cockpit enclosure), a switch from the anti-ship to the land-attack role with a larger load of different weapon types, and two different turbojet engine types: the early models were powered by the Wright J65 (an Americanised and not altogether successful version of a British engine, the Armstrong Siddeley Sapphire), but in new-build models from the A-4E the standard engine became the Pratt & Whitney J52.

The definitive late-production model was the A-4M Skyhawk II with the powerplant of one J52-P-408A turbojet rated at 11,200lb (5,080kg) st, span of 27ft 6in (8.38m), length of 40 ft 3.25 in (12.27 m), empty weight of 10,465 lb (4747 kg), maximum take-off weight of 27,420lb (12,437kg), maximum speed of 670mph; 1,078km/h) at optimum altitude, initial climb rate of 8,440ft (2,572m) per minute, service ceiling of 49,000ft (14,935m), and range of about 920 miles (1,480km) with the maximum external weapons load. This last comprises 9,155lb (4,153kg) of stores as diverse as 'dumb' bombs of the free-fall or retarded types, cluster bombs, dispenser weapons, rocket-launcher pods, cannon pods, and air-to-surface missiles. The Skyhawk also carries a fixed forward-firing armament of two 20mm Mk 12 cannon or, in a number of export aircraft, two 30mm DEFA cannon.

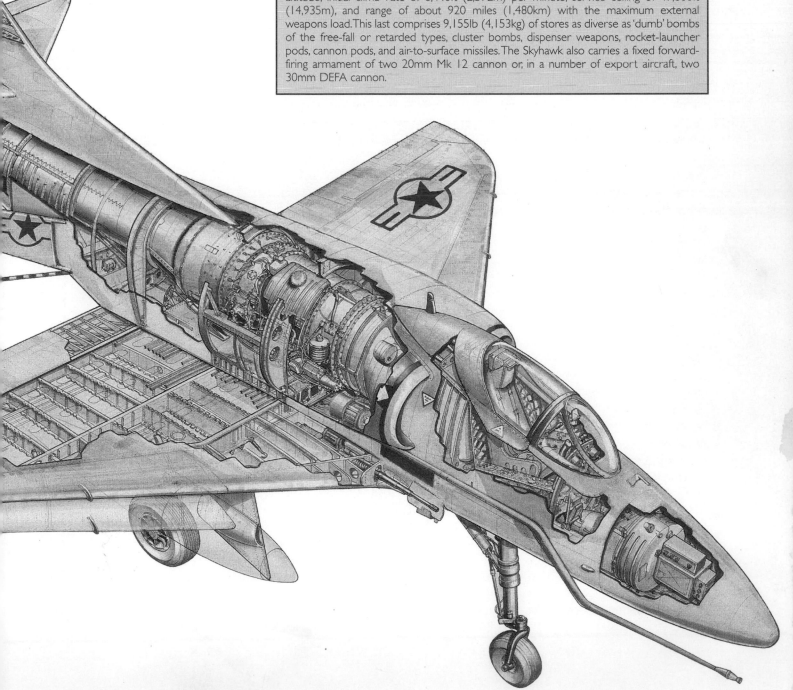

Pakistan bought a large number of ex-Australian Mirage IIIs during the early 1990s, with a view to supplementing its current fleet of Mirages with an upgraded variant.

A notable factor in fighter design since the early 1950s has been the wide range of tasks which operators expect of their smaller combat aircraft. Up to the middle of World War II, it was possible to build a combat aeroplane for one specific role, but development costs have since been prohibitively high for such development to be considered by any country other than one of the two superpowers. The tendency has been towards the creation of multi-role aircraft, and this tendency was discernible even during World War II in the evolution of supremely versatile types such as the de Havilland Mosquito and Junkers Ju 88.

Each role demands its own electronics package and specialised weapons, but this fact has actually eased the designers' task. Providing the electronics packages for all-weather interception, reconnaissance and ground-attack roles can be accommodated in the same fuselage, the basic aeroplane can be used in a number of roles. Reduced to its simplest terms, the designer's task from the mid-1950s until recently has been to produce an aeroplane capable of high performance at all altitudes and in all conditions, but with the ability to carry a heavy offensive load on the exterior hardpoints and sufficient internal volume for accommodation of the relevant avionics. Although simple in concept, such design is vastly complex in practice, and has been complicated further by the realisation that missiles have some disadvantages in combat. Internally mounted guns, with all their bulky ammunition and fire-control radars, must now be designed into the airframe.

Advanced combat aircraft are so prohibitively expensive that the economies of the United Kingdom and France were severely strained by the development and production of machines such as the Lightning and Mirage.

Other European countries, apart from Sweden, could not match this expenditure, and so bought aircraft from one of the main producers, or concentrated on less advanced types with limited capabilities.

Italy produced the lightweight G91 close-support aircraft, and developed its two most important turbojet-powered trainers into useful but limited light-attack types: the single-seat attack version of the MB-326 sold moderately well, but the comparable version of the MB-339 (an evolutionary development of the MB-326 with a revised forward fuselage offering vertically stepped accommodation) failed to attract any purchasers. This has been a growing trend since the mid-1960s, followed by countries such as the

Designed and developed with considerable speed in the period immediately after World War II but still in modest service with a number of countries, the Ilyushin Il-28 'Beagle' was planned as a tactical light bomber with a powerplant of two simple turbojet engines, and was therefore in the same basic class as the English Electric Canberra. There was little complexity in the design, which has a three-man crew, a straight wing but swept tail surfaces, tricycle landing gear, two Klimov VK-1 turbojets each rated at 5,792lb (2,700kg) st which are installed in underwing nacelles, and a primary armament of 4,409lb (2000kg) of bombs carried in a lower-fuselage weapons bay. The gun armament comprises four 23mm NR-23 cannon, two of them fixed forward-firing weapons in the nose whilst two are trainable weapons in the manned tail turret.

United Kingdom, France, Spain, Romania and the former Yugoslavia. Such machines are still sold to Third World nations as primary combat aircraft, and provide a secondary attack capability for the home air forces. Virtually no trainer designed since 1970, even in the United States and the USSR, has lacked this secondary attack capability.

The US Air Force's inventory of modern combat aircraft designed between the late 1940s and late 1950s, ranging from the F-86 Sabre to the Convair F-102 Delta Dagger and F-106 Delta Dart interceptors, was impressive. It was then matched by just one truly superlative type, the McDonnell (later McDonnell Douglas) F-4 Phantom II multi-role fighter, developed for the US Navy but then adopted for the US Air Force. Design began in 1954, and by 1960 the type was recognised as the best all-round combat aeroplane developed in the United States since the end of World War II. With a lowering, aggressive appearance, the Phantom II was first conceived as a carrierborne attack aeroplane but was built in prototype form as a two-seat carrierborne fleet defence fighter (the first aircraft capable of undertaking the whole interception mission without support from surface ships). It then evolved into strike, attack, close support, electronic pathfinder, defence suppression and reconnaissance forms, and is still used by a number of Western air forces apart from those of the United States, where the type is due for retirement from US Air Force service in the second half of the 1990s.

The lessons of combat in Vietnam during the late 1960s and early 1970s led to the development of a new model with fixed gun armament, in the form of the redoubtable 20mm Vulcan six-barrelled rotary cannon capable of a rate of fire in the order of 6,000 rounds per minute This convinced the governments of most countries of the need for fighters with a fixed gun

In the early 1950s NATO became very concerned about the vulnerability to missile and bomb attack of the large air bases required for its increasingly capable, complex and expensive warplanes. The organisation therefore sponsored a number of design competitions to produce lighter, less complex and less expensive warplanes that could operate from fields or strips of undamaged road in times of crisis. The only one of these types to enter full production in its planned form was the Fiat G91 light-attack fighter adopted in Italy (its parent country) and West Germany but later passed on to Portugal. In its original forms as the G91R reconnaissance and light attack fighter and G91T combat-capable advanced trainer, the type had a powerplant of one Bristol Orpheus turbojet, but later development resulted in the G91Y with a powerplant of two General Electric J85 turbojets for improved performance and greater flight safety.

armament, and further evidence was provided by Israeli aircraft in the 'Six-Day War', when cannon proved as useful as guided missiles, especially at the low speeds and short ranges at which air combat was joined.

Immediately after the end of World War II, the main strength of the US Navy's air arm lay with piston-engined types such as the Grumman F8F Bearcat fighter, the Vought F4U Corsair fighter and fighter-bomber, and the Douglas AD Skyraider attack bomber, which was still flying over Vietnam in the early 1970s. Interim turbojet-powered types were under development, however, and by the early 1950s the US Navy and US Marine Corps had accepted a number of new aircraft such as the Grumman F9F fighter (in its straight-winged Panther and swept-wing Cougar forms), the McDonnell F2H Banshee and F3H Demon fighters, and the Douglas F3D Skyknight all-weather fighter.

Seen in company with a pair of intercepting McDonnell Douglas F-4 Phantom II fighters, the Tupolev Tu-95 'Bear' was a remarkable technical and operational triumph. First flown in prototype form during 1954, the type was planned as a less advanced back-up to the Myasishchyev M-4 'Bison' turbojet-powered strategic bomber. Range was always a problem with the thirsty turbojets of the day, so the Tu-95 was planned with the odd combination of fully swept flying surfaces and a powerplant of four extremely potent turboprop engines each driving an eight-blade contra-rotating propeller unit. As a result the Tu-95 offered near-jet speed together with considerably greater range, and the type was therefore placed in large-scale production, eventually exceeding that of the disappointing M-4 by a considerable degree. The Tu-95 also proved to be very versatile, the original bomber version soon being supplemented by missile-carrying models with large stand-off missiles, multi-sensor reconnaissance models optimised for the maritime role, and maritime patrol models optimised for the anti-submarine role. Later production aircraft were to the somewhat improved Tu-142 standard that was phased out of production only in the early 1990s after delivery in anti-submarine and cruise missile launch platform versions.

Later in the 1950s, the Douglas A3D Skywarrior attack bomber and A4D Skyhawk light-attack aeroplane appeared, and the US Navy moved into the supersonic age with the Vought F8U Crusader fighter whose configuration was later scaled-down to create the LTV A-7 Corsair II strike and attack aeroplane. The largest and heaviest carrierborne aeroplane, the Mach 2 North American A3J Vigilante attack bomber, entered service in 1960.

All these aircraft operated in Vietnam, and constant updating of their engines and avionics kept them in the forefront of military technology well into the 1970s. The US Navy types were resilient and versatile machines, disproving the theory that turbojet-powered aircraft and their avionics would be susceptible to battle damage. The only US Air Force aeroplane to match the Navy machines was the F-105, and this had serviceability problems that would never have been permitted in a carrierborne combat aeroplane.

By the 1970s, the only other countries to develop carrierborne aircraft were France and the United Kingdom. Re-formed towards the end of World War II, the French naval air arm initially operated American naval aircraft, and in the mid-1990s still operates the Crusader, which was redesignated as the F-8 in 1962 as part of the rationalisation of the US forces' previously separate tri-service designation systems into a single system. From the early

McDonnell Douglas F-4 Phantom II

THE F-4 Phantom II must be considered as one of the greatest warplanes of all time. The type has been used with great success in a number of wars and has revealed great 'developability' in its primary and increasing number of secondary roles. Angular, brutish and pugnacious in appearance, the Phantom II is notable for its very good performance, reliable twin-engined powerplant, good agility despite its large size and considerable weight, and overall amenability to improvement.

The original F-4A version was a pilot-production model that entered service only in small numbers, so the first major models were the F-4B and RF-4B carrierborne fighter and reconnaissance models. There followed the F-4C and RF-4C versions of the F-4B and RF-4C for the US Air Force, the F-4D more fully optimized USAF model, the F-4E and RF-4E definitive land-based fighter and reconnaissance models with the inbuilt cannon armament lacking from the previous models, the F-4F air-superiority fighter for the West German air force, the F-4G 'Advanced Wild Weasel' defence-suppression rebuild of the F-4E, the F-4J improved carrierborne model with all-round improvements, the F-4K and F-4M anglicised versions for the Fleet Air Arm and RAF with a powerplant of two Rolls-Royce Spey turbofans in place of the otherwise standard General Electric J79 turbojets, and the F-4S equivalent to the F-4J produced as F-4B conversions.

The F-4E may be regarded as the definitive model. This has a crew of two (pilot and systems operator), an armament of one 20mm M61A1 Vulcan six-barrel cannon and up to 16,000lb (7257kg) of highly diverse unguided and guided weapons carried on one under-fuselage and four underwing hardpoints, a powerplant of two J79-GE-17A turbojets each rated at 17,900lb (8,120kg) st with afterburning, maximum speed of 1,500mph (2,414km/h) of Mach 2.2 at high altitude, initial climb rate of 28,000ft (8,534m) per second, service ceiling of more than 60,000ft (19,685m), and range of 1,750 miles (2,817km) without external weapons.

1960s, however, the Dassault Etendard IVM proved itself a more than adequate carrierborne attack aircraft, and the Breguet 1050 Alizé (tradewind) has also served well in the anti-submarine role.

The Fleet Air Arm (FAA) of the Royal Navy possessed few high-performance aircraft during World War II, apart from converted landplanes such as the Supermarine Seafire adaptation of the Spitfire. In the years after 1945, it soldiered on with piston-engined types such as the Hawker Sea Fury fighter, Fairey Firefly reconnaissance fighter and Fairey Barracuda torpedo bomber, as well as a number of more advanced American aircraft such as the Grumman Avenger that was operated in the airborne early warning (AEW) role. The FAA acquired its first turbine-powered types in the early 1950s: the Supermarine Attacker and Hawker Sea Hawk fighters, and the Fairey Gannet anti-submarine aeroplane which was powered by a turboprop engine, like its French contemporary, the Alizé.

By the late 1950s, three swept-wing aircraft designs were under development for the FAA, and entered service late in the 1950s and early in the 1960s. These were the Supermarine Scimitar interceptor and strike fighter, the de Havilland (later Hawker Siddeley) Sea Vixen interceptor and the Blackburn (later Hawker Siddeley) Buccaneer strike aeroplane. The Buccaneer was a particularly good machine, with excellent performance 'on the deck' through careful aerodynamic design, and first-class landing characteristics as a result of a 'super-circulation' boundary-layer control system.

Despite its many virtues, the Buccaneer was long resisted by the RAF, which wanted the considerably more advanced British Aircraft Corporation (BAC) TSR-2 tactical strike and reconnaissance aeroplane. In the mid-1960s, however, the RAF reluctantly agreed to accept surviving ex-FAA aircraft when the Royal Navy's force of large aircraft-carriers was retired later in the decade. The TSR-2 project had been cancelled, and much to its surprise the RAF found the Buccaneer to be a truly great aeroplane. It was then ordered in large numbers, the last examples being retired only in 1994.

The USSR's air force moved into the Mach 2 era with the Mikoyan-Gurevich MiG-21 'Fishbed' fighter, designed to supersede the highly successful MiG-19. Small and compact for a Mach 2 aircraft, the MiG-21 had a delta wing but conventional, highly-swept tail surfaces, and proved both popular and successful. Lacking the size, weight and versatility of the Phantom II, the MiG-21 was designed for the short-range interception mission in clear weather conditions, using ground-controlled interception (GCI) techniques. Total production in the USSR, several Warsaw Pact countries and India numbered more than 6,500 aircraft, and an additional large but unspecified quantity has been built in China as the Chengdu J-7 series, which has in turn spawned the export-oriented F-7M Airguard derivative with its large proportion of Western avionics.

Although conceived for the clear-weather interception role and first flown in 1955 with comparatively light armament, the MiG-21 was successfully evolved into a limited all-weather type capable of interception and ground-attack roles as a result of upgraded avionics and additional armament capability. The MiG-21 family also included several reconnaissance models and three tandem-seat operational conversion trainers, and during its long production career the MiG-21 was built in many variants with three basic engine types, increasingly large dorsal spines allowing a major increase in internal fuel capacity and, in the last model, a completely re-engineered airframe.

The MiG-21 series was built in larger numbers than any other Soviet warplane since World War II, and was used by virtually every Soviet ally,

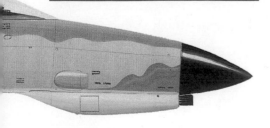

client and satellite. Although the type had disappeared from Soviet first-line service by the early 1990s, the type survives in large numbers with the air forces of most other Soviet-bloc countries, and the mid-1990s are witnessing a scrambled contest as the Russian parent organisation competes with several Western countries for the lucrative upgrade of these obsolescent aircraft. The update requested by most operators is concerned mainly with the MiG-21's avionics and weapons capabilities, and although India has opted for a Russian upgrade with Russian radar, it has also specified Western items for a large proportion of other features. It is likely that many of the other upgrade customers will follow a similar course.

In its heyday the Soviet fighter, because of its small size and low wing loading, could usually outfly contemporary American aircraft, and the MiG-19 helped to demonstrate that the art of dogfighting, a useful element of the fighter pilot's inventory of skills, had not disappeared. Part of the MiG-21's undoubted export popularity lay in its relative cheapness; in general, this trim fighter cost between one-quarter and one-third of the price for a Phantom II.

The nearest Soviet equivalent to the mighty F-105 Thunderchief as an attack aeroplane was a series of sturdy swept-wing designs originating in the design bureau of Pavel Sukhoi. The Su-7 'Fitter' series equipped most of the air forces in the Soviet sphere of influence, but although it has much the same performance as the F-105, the Su-7 cannot carry the same offensive load and is also notably deficient in range even when carrying two drop tanks in place of disposable armament. The Su-7 series may be regarded as a short-range close-support fighter whereas the F-105 was a long-range strike and attack fighter. In its milieu, however, the Su-7 was unrivalled until the late 1980s, for it was very fast at low level, monumentally strong, and a superb weapon platform because of its low gust response.

Even though the Su-7 was a superb operational aeroplane, especially in its

The Breguet (now Dassault) Alizé is typical of the type of small anti-submarine aeroplane forced on lesser naval air arms by the modest size of their aircraft-carriers. Powered by a single Rolls-Royce Dart turboprop, whose considerable fuel economy offers useful endurance, the Alizé has a crew of three, carries moderately advanced electronics, and can lift a useful weapons load in its lower-fuselage weapons bay and on underwing hardpoints. The type is operated only by the French and Indian navies.

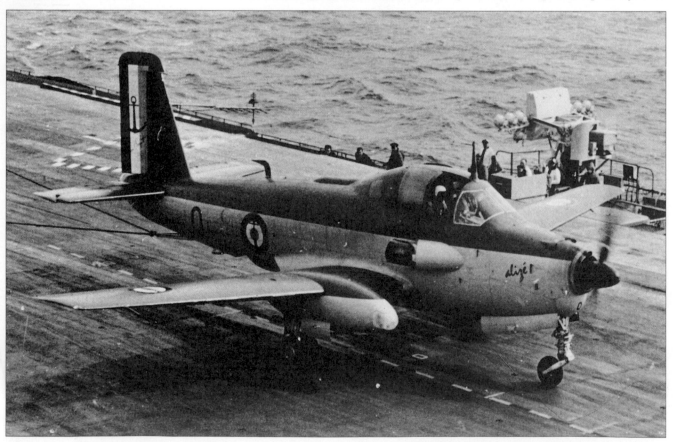

An altogether more sophisticated approach to the problems of carrierborne anti-submarine operations was possible for the US Navy, which operates a greater number of aircraft-carriers all with considerably larger flight-decks. The solution for the US Navy is represented by the Lockheed S-3 Viking, which it achieves extraordinary success in the difficult feat of packing maximum electronics, weapons and fuel in an airframe capable of undertaking long-endurance missions yet small enough (with its wings folded) to be carried in useful numbers on aircraft-carriers packed with a host of other warplane types. The Viking is powered by two fuel-economical General Electric TF34 turbofan engines pod-mounted below wings that contain large integral fuel tanks, and the basically rectangular-section fuselage carries the crew of four, a mass of very advanced electronic equipment (radar, magnetic anomaly detector, acoustic data-processing equipment and associated droppable sonobuoys, electronic support measures equipment and the systems to combine their data into a complete tactical picture) and a lower-fuselage weapons bay for a decisive quantity of anti-submarine weaponry that can be complemented by missiles such as the McDonnell Douglas AGM-84 Harpoon anti-ship missile on two underwing hardpoints.

later variants with short take-off and landing (STOL) capability which enabled operation from semi-prepared airstrips immediately behind the front line, the Soviet air forces were unhappy with the type's very poor payload/range performance, and from 1960 the design bureau started work on a variable-geometry derivative offering improved payload/range performance. For a combination of technical and production reasons it was decided to pivot only the outer half of each wing, but this proved adequate to transform the basic close-support fighter's payload/range performance. The resulting aeroplane entered service in 1971 as the Su-17 'Fitter-C', which was also produced in differently engined Su-20 and Su-22 forms. With the outer wing sections in their minimum-sweep position, the Su-17 series aircraft had much improved field performance and greater tactical radius; and with the wings in the maximum-sweep position, speed was comparable with that of the Su-7. The net result was that the Su-17 series could carry 250 per cent more payload over 30 per cent greater tactical radius.

Unlike the other half of the Mikoyan-Gurevich prototype series, which did not lead to a production swept-wing aeroplane, the other half of the Sukhoi prototype series resulted in a production aeroplane with a tailed-delta layout. The first of this series was the Su-9 'Fishpot' interceptor that was reserved for Soviet use from the time of its introduction in mid-1959. From 1966, it was complemented by the improved Su-11 'Fishpot', and production of the two models totalled some 2,000 aircraft. These were gradually supplanted from the early 1970s by the Su-15 'Flagon', which was probably designed to replace the Yakovlev Yak-28P 'Firebar' Mach 1.9 interceptor. The Su-15 was altogether a more advanced interceptor, offering Mach 2+ performance both as a result of its more refined airframe incorporating a large measure of area-ruling, and its considerably more potent twin-engined powerplant aspirated via wing-root inlets rather than the earlier types' nose inlet. This latter fact allowed the incorporation of a much superior interception radar with its antenna in the large nose radome. The last Su-15 interceptors were retired only in the late 1980s.

Also in service with the USSR's forces until this time was the Tupolev Tu-28P 'Fiddler', the largest interceptor fighter in service anywhere in the world, and intended primarily for poor-weather operations in the USSR's northern regions. These areas were poorly equipped with air bases, but lay on the optimum trans-polar route that would probably have been used by American strategic bombers attacking the USSR. The only way to provide effective patrol and interception capabilities in these regions was therefore through the development of a moderately supersonic interceptor with an airframe large enough to carry considerable fuel, a two-man crew, an extremely powerful radar system, and four large long-range air-to-air missiles.

Not all the energy of the world's military aircraft designers went into the evolution of fighters, however. With the destruction of Hiroshima and Nagasaki, the strategic bomber had proved its value beyond all doubt. The invention of an immensely destructive device such as the A-bomb (fission or nuclear bomb) opened the possibility of true strategic air power in the form of just a few aircraft, each crewed by less than a dozen men. The theories of men such as Douhet, Mitchell and Trenchard in the 1920s were finally proved by the destruction of Hiroshima and Nagasaki, and their concept of strategic bombing as the arbiter of war was made still more terrible by the development of the even more powerful H-bomb (fusion or thermonuclear bomb) shortly after the end of World War II.

It was inevitable that these weapons should come to dominate military thinking in the late 1940s. It was assumed that long-range guided missiles, based on the German V-2 of World War II, would eventually be developed as a delivery system for such weapons, but in the short term the only practical solution seemed to lie with the long-range manned bomber, and then the long-range unmanned bomber, which was essentially a surface-to-surface missile of the type that would now be classified as a cruise missile, albeit of considerably larger size than anything in service today. The manned

Designed at much the same time as the Mikoyan-Gurevich MiG-21 'Fishbed' lightweight tactical fighter, the Sukhoi Su-7 'Fitter' was also designed as a tactical fighter but emerged as a somewhat larger and heavier type optimized for the attack-fighter role. The type saw extensive service with the USSR and its allies and clients between the 1960s and 1980s, and acquired something of a mixed reputation. On the credit side, the Su-7 was recognised as rugged, fast at low level, and an extremely good weapons platform, while on the debit side were the type's extremely thirsty Lyul'ka AL-7 afterburning turbojet engine and limited external weapons carriage capability. The former meant that even with two drop tanks the tactical radius was exceptionally short while the latter meant that, even before two hardpoints were lost to the inevitable drop tanks, only a very modest weapons load could be lifted. The situation was improved somewhat in the later Su-17 'Fitter' series, which adopted hinged outer wing panels to improve field and cruise performance, resulting in lowered fuel consumption.

bomber, therefore, became the single most important type of weapon in the arsenals of the United States, the USSR and the United Kingdom, the only three countries with nuclear weapons in the 1950s. Heavy bombers were always designed with the capacity to carry such weapons, even if the specific type of bomb had not been fully developed at the time.

The only turbojet-powered bomber in operational service when the war ended was a German type, the Arado Ar 234 Blitz (lightning). The Germans had been experimenting with several other types of turbojet-powered bomber, most notably the Junkers Ju 287. This extraordinary aeroplane had a forward-swept wing, and the powerplant comprised four turbojets which were installed as two under the wing and two on the sides of the forward fuselage. Fascinating experimental data on the use of forward-swept wings as a means of combating the worst effects of high-speed compression were obtained by the Americans and the Soviets, but as yet no military aircraft with forward-swept wings has entered production.

By 1946, both the superpowers had instituted top-priority programmes to develop a strategic bomber capable of carrying nuclear bombs over very long ranges. At the same time, the USSR was abandoning its virtually exclusive concentration on tactical air power for a more mixed approach. This reflected the fact that while the Soviet air force had shown itself to be the most powerful support arm in the world, aiding the Red Army in its massive pushes into Germany, the Soviet leaders had been greatly impressed by the devastation wrought on Germany and Japan by the combined Western bomber offensive. The Soviets began by building the Tupolev Tu-4 'Bull', a reverse-engineered derivative of the Superfortress, as their first strategic bomber type.

The United States had become convinced during World War II that it needed a completely new generation of bombers, and had therefore begun a large-scale research and development programme. Yet just after the war, before the new bombers could be placed in service, the most important aircraft in the Strategic Air Command (SAC) was the Boeing B-50 development of the B-29, with more advanced systems, better armament and uprated engines. Even so, the very fact of the SAC's formation indicated the importance attached to the United States' concept of nuclear strategic bombing.

The B-50 was essentially an interim type, pending the arrival of one of the oddest and most controversial aeroplanes of all time, the Convair B-36. This had its origins in the American decision of 1943 to build a fleet of advanced bombers, but design and prototype construction were delayed initially by the more immediate demands of World War II. When this important programme was later undertaken as a matter of high priority, it was soon discovered that the pace of technical development in this forcing period of history had been so fast, that the planned type was already on the verge of obsolescence in all features but its payload/range performance, which ensured that a heavy bomb load could be delivered over intercontinental ranges. Development and procurement of the B-36 continued, however, and the type entered service in the late 1940s. With a wing spanning no less than 230ft (70.1m), the monstrous B-36 was powered by six 3,500hp radial piston engines buried in the wings, driving pusher propellers located behind the wing trailing edges.

At a time when advanced turbojet-powered fighters were opening the possibility of combat operations at high subsonic speeds, the B-36 was judged too slow for survivability in its basic piston-engined form. Thus the B-36D featured a boosted powerplant, with the original piston engines supplemented by four turbojet engines in pods, each accommodating two

Soviet Parallel Design Concepts

IN December 1949, Pavel Sukhoi and about half of the team of his designers were subordinated to the over-pressed Tupolev bureau, Sukhoi himself was allowed to continue a measure of basic research and collaborated with the Central Aerodynamics and Hydrodynamics Institute (TsAGI), in the development of two basic design concepts.

These were both tailed types, one based on a conventional wing swept (the S type) and the other on a delta wing (the T type). The first of at least five S-1 research aircraft flew in mid-1955, and in the following two years the series was used for a major programme of research and development.

In the early 1950s the Soviet air forces issued a requirement for an advanced fighter to counter the first two of the US Air Force's 'century' series fighters, namely the North American F-100 Super Sabre and McDonnell F-101 Voodoo. The result was a series of warplanes that were larger and heavier than their Western counterparts, with the required performance provided by a higher-rated powerplant drawing its fuel from a relatively smaller internal capacity.

Designs to meet the Soviet air forces' requirement were drawn up by the Mikoyan-Gurevich and Sukhoi bureaux, the former offering the I-380 that was broadly similar to the Sukhoi design in configuration and powerplant. Sukhoi's response to the requirement was based on his team's experience with the experimental configurations mentioned above, and the basic S-1 was accordingly evolved into a more advanced form with an area-ruled airframe incorporating flying surfaces characterised by a leading-edge sweep angle of 62 degrees, slab tailplane halves, artificial feel in the powered control surfaces, four air brakes on the rear fuselage, an improved wing with kinked trailing edges for greater area, a less tapered nose providing a larger inlet for greater airflow in combination with suck-in auxiliary doors, a translating inlet centrebody containing the antenna for the SRD-5 intercept radar, a clamshell cockpit canopy, and a ribbon-type brake chute in a box under the rear fuselage.

The Convair B-58 Hustler was the world's first supersonic bomber. The main conceptual problem facing the designers of this aircraft was that the internal carriage of the nuclear weapon payload and all the fuel for both outward and inward legs of the mission would result in an aeroplane so large that supersonic performance would not really be possible even with the new and potentially superb General Electric J79 afterburning turbojet that was the best available engine for the bomber. The solution that offered itself to the design team was elegant yet daring: create a small bomber without internal weapons accommodation or fuel for more than one leg of the mission, and add both these in the form of a large and nicely streamlined pod carried under the fuselage and carrying both the nuclear payload and the fuel for the outward leg of the mission. The whole assembly was supersonic, but over the target the pod containing the bomb and now-surplus fuel tankage was dropped, reducing the weight and drag of the bomber for higher exit speed and a return to base on the internal fuel tankage. The B-58 entered service in the early 1960s, and provided a very high degree of capability although only at the expense of complex maintenance. The type was withdrawn from service in 1970.

side-by-side engines, attached under the outer wing panels. This boosted the maximum speed to 435mph (700km/h), considerably below the figure attainable by current fighters, but which, in conjunction with the bomber's prodigious defensive armament of paired 20mm cannon, was deemed to offer at least a measure of survivability.

Although the B-36 had the neccessary range of 7,500 miles (12,070km) for global missions, the US Air Force soon appreciated that the very size of the aeroplane was a hindrance to its survivability and therefore its likely success in combat. The B-36's radar signature was enormous, for example, and this made the type highly detectable even by the comparatively primitive ground-based radars then available to the Soviets.

The Americans reasoned that they should replace the B-36 with a smaller, faster and less detectable bomber. But a smaller airframe also entailed reduced fuel capacity and thus restricted range at a time when the SAC was being developed as the United States' primary method of strategic power projection. The answer lay in aerial refuelling, which had been attempted as early as the 1920s, but was now being brought to an acceptable operational capability by the British and the Americans. Britain opted for the hose-and-drogue type of refuelling, in which the receiver aeroplane noses its refuelling probe into a basket trailed at the end of a hose by the tanker, whilst the Americans developed the flying boom, which an operator in the tanker 'flies' into a receptacle of the receiver aeroplane.

The B-36 was an interim type, and was replaced from the early 1950s by the remarkable Boeing B-47 Stratojet and Boeing B-52 Stratofortress turbojet-powered bombers operating in the medium and heavy strategic

Changing Concepts of Bomber Design

THE imminent debut of turbojet-powered fighters in the middle stages of World War II rightly persuaded the US Army Air Force in 1943 that, in the future, bombers would only survive against turbojet-powered fighters if they adopted a similar powerplant for much higher speed and service ceiling. By 1944, five companies were involved in the design of jet-powered bombers, their initial thoughts being centred on conventional (and thus straight-winged) aircraft with turbojets in place of piston engines. Boeing proposed its Model 424 that was in essence a scaled-down Model 345 (B-29 Superfortress) with four turbojets in podded pairs under the wings. The proposal failed to interest the USAAF, and the company revised the concept into the Model 432 with all four engines buried in the fuselage. The new proposal aroused limited interest, and Boeing was contracted for design definition and a mock-up of this XB-47.

As the company was proceeding with these initial steps, a team of its designers and engineers was allowed in the summer of 1945 to visit captured German factories and research centres, in the process discovering the advantages of swept flying surfaces for aircraft of high subsonic performance. Boeing therefore recast the Model 432 as the Model 448 with a thin wing characterised by a quarter-chord sweep angle of 35 degrees. At this stage the USAAF raised objections to the grouping of the engines in the fuselage, where they would be highly vulnerable to disablement by a single hit, and Boeing thus recast the design as the Model 450 with six engines located under the wings as two podded pairs inboard and two podded singletons outboard, each pod unit being placed below and ahead of the wing leading edge in a position that interfered minimally with the flow of air over the wing and also offered structural advantages in reducing the long, thin wing's tendency to bow under load.

This was the definitive design, and was optimised for the carriage of current nuclear weapons, which were both large and heavy, in a large weapon bay on high-altitude missions to attack area targets deep in enemy territory. The Model 450 thus began to mature as a high-altitude type with a crew of three including two pilots in a fighter-type cockpit, all-swept flying surfaces including a cantilever high-set wing of laminar-flow section, and bicycle-type landing gear with tandem twin-wheel units under the fuselage (fore and aft of the weapon bay) and small single-wheel stabiliser units extending from the underside of the twin-engine pods. The first of two XB-47 (Model 450-3-3) prototypes flew in December 1947 with a powerplant of six General Electric J35-GE-2 turbojets each rated at 3,750lb (1,701kg) st, while the second prototype had a powerplant of six General Electric J47-GE-3 turbojets each rated at 5,000lb (2,268kg) st. The indifferent power of these engines advocated the use of booster rockets for take-off, and the XB-47s had provision for 16 solid-propellant RATO units in the fuselage sides aft of the wing. The new bomber clearly possessed exceptional potential and the US Air Force, as the USAAF had now become, ordered the type as the B-47 Stratojet, which entered service in the early 1950s as the USA's first turbojet-powered strategic bomber.

roles respectively. The B-47 was a version developed from one of five turbine-powered experimental bomber designs ordered by the US Army Air Force in 1943. A superbly clean and sleek type whose swept-wing design was finalised only after the Americans had digested the implications of German research data captured at the end of World War II, the Stratojet revealed how the aerodynamics hitherto applied only to small fighters could be successfully used on a large aeroplane with its wings swept at 35 degrees. Although it was classified as a medium bomber, its range of 4,000 miles (6,437km/h) and maximum speed of 600mph (966km/h) made the B-47, with a bomb load of 22,000lb (9,979kg), a far more formidable combat aeroplane than the larger and theoretically more devastating B-36.

The United Kingdom at last entered the field of strategic nuclear bombing with turbojet-engined aircraft. The first of these, essentially an interim type, was the Vickers Valiant, a four-engined machine with pleasing lines, and the first of the United Kingdom's 'V-bombers' to enter service. The Valiant's performance was limited by its intermediate design, which resulted in a wing of only modest sweep, but the type was used for developing the tactics of British nuclear bombing, and also for testing the British fission and fusion weapons.

The Americans followed the Stratojet with the B-52 Stratofortress, which entered service with the SAC in 1955. The family likeness to the B-47 was immediately apparent, but the B-52 is an altogether larger and more powerful aeroplane with a maximum speed of 660mph (1,062km/h), a range of 10,000 miles (16,093km), and a normal bomb load of up to 27,000lb (12,247kg) of nuclear weapons carried internally, that can be increased in some models to a maximum of 75,000lb (34,020kg) of conventional weapons carried internally, and externally. Powered by eight engines in four twin-engined under-wing pods, and fitted with the same type of landing gear arrangement as the B-47, the B-52 has proved to be an enormously versatile strategic bomber, used to such devastating effect for tactical bombing in the Vietnam War. In 1961, the B-52G variant entered service with the capability

The demands of night and all-weather interception of heavy bombers during the late 1940s and early 1950s presented designers with acute problems: high speed was necessary to ensure rapid interception, so turbojet propulsion was required; long endurance was essential for sustained patrols, so a substantial, fuel-filled airframe was inevitable; and the airborne interception radar of the period was bulky and needed a dedicated operator, so still further demands were made on airframe size and weight. This meant that almost all of the night- and all-weather fighters of the period were large machines with a twin-engined powerplant to ensure that performance was not adversely affected by the drag and weight of the airframe. A typical example of this trend was the Gloster Javelin, a British fighter carrying its radar in the large nose, and with a delta wing of great area and considerable thickness to accommodate the engines and large quantity of fuel. Knowledge of the aerodynamic factors associated with delta wings was still poor at this time, so the Javelin was also given a large horizontal tail surface mounted at the head of the vertical surface to provide full longitudinal control.

to carry and launch two North American AGM-28 Hound Dog nuclear-tipped air-to-surface missiles, and from 1981 the last two variants (the B-52G and turbofan-powered B-52H) were revised for carriage of the Boeing AGM-86 air-launched cruise missile. Although the B-52 was supplanted as the SAC's most important strategic bomber from 1986 by the Rockwell B-1 Lancer, the type is still in comparatively widespread service as a conventional bomber and sea-control aeroplane.

The United Kingdom's small fleet of Valiant bombers had to be grounded and scrapped in 1964 because of fatigue problems, but by this time the RAF's two primary V-bombers were in service. These were the Avro Vulcan, the first large delta-wing aeroplane to enter service anywhere in the world, and the more conventional Handley Page Victor whose 'crescent' flying surfaces featured a sweep angle that gradually reduced from root to tip. Both of these long-range heavy bombers (medium range by US standards) resulted from a requirement drafted as early as 1946, but official vacillation resulted in both types going into production, with a consequent increase in aircraft unit costs and a complete doubling of training, spares and procedures. The only redeeming feature of this duplication was that the Victor emerged as an excellent tanker, and the Vulcan as a low-level attack bomber. The last few Vulcans were rescued from retirement in 1982 to participate in the Falklands campaign, when very long flight-refuelled missions were flown from a forward base on Ascension Island in the South Atlantic. The last Victor tankers were retired only in the mid-1990s when their airframe hours were exhausted after intensive operations in the 1991 UN-led campaign to expel the Iraqi occupiers from Kuwait.

Convair B-36 'Peacemaker'

AFTER World War II, the US Air Force invited both Boeing and Consolidated to prepare design studies for a bomber able to reach 450mph (724km/h) at 25,000ft (7,620m), cover a range of 12,000 miles (19,312km) with a bomb load of 4,000lb (1,814kg), deliver a bomb load of 10,000lb (4,536kg) to a radius of 3,400 miles (5,472km), and reach an altitude of 35,000ft (10,670m).

Consolidated had already considered such a type with a tail unit carrying endplate vertical surfaces and with a powerplant of six pusher engines to improve airflow over the wings, and submitted this Model 35 design in May 1941. The company refined this design during the summer of 1941 as Boeing (together with Douglas and Northrop) pressed ahead with rival concepts. In November 1941 the USAAF contracted with Consolidated for two XB-36 prototypes that were to be delivered in 1944. The definition of the design resulted in considerable growth of size and weight, requiring the use of six huge R-4360 radials buried in the wings where they could be reached for inflight maintenance and were supplied with fuel from an internal capacity of 17,583 Imp gal (79,932.5litres) in six wing-mounted tanks. The envisaged bomb load was 42,000lb (19,051kg) carried in four bomb bays below a tunnel 85ft (25.91m) long for the wheeled cart that moved on twin rails to provide a means of transfer between the two pressurised compartments (forward crew and rear gunners' sections).

Up to the summer of 1944 the whole programme was seriously delayed by its low priority, but the high cost to the US forces of capturing the Mariana Islands to provide the bases needed for the strategic bombing of Japan by Boeing B-29 Superfortresses then persuaded the USAAF to afford the B-36 a higher priority. The first XB-36 flew in August 1946 with a flush flight-deck canopy and main landing gear units each carrying a single wheel 9ft 2in (2.79m) in diameter. These units exerted so great a ground pressure that there were only three airfields in the continental USA with runways offering concrete of the required 22in (0.56m) thickness; the XB-36 was therefore revised with a four-wheel bogie on each main landing gear unit, reducing the required concrete thickness to 13.5in (0.34m). The machine was also fitted with the raised flightdeck glazing that was adopted as standard, and took to the air in this revised form during June 1948.

The Convair B-58 Hustler supersonic bomber entered service in 1960. Powered by four podded turbojets, the delta-winged Hustler was capable of 1,385mph (2,229km/h) and had a service ceiling of 60,000ft (18,290m). To maintain a clean fuselage for minimum drag and maximum speed, the designers placed both the weapon load and the fuel for the outward leg of the mission in a streamlined pod under the fuselage. This pod was designed to be jettisoned over the target, enabling the unencumbered bomber to fly home at maximum speed.

The Hustler was not entirely successful, however, and in the late 1960s its task assumed by the General Dynamics F-111 series. The first major combat aeroplane to enter service with a variable-geometry wing planform, the F-111 was planned for the US Air Force, but a subsequent political decision dictated its development as a carrierborne fleet air-defence fighter for the

US Navy, as the use of a single airframe/powerplant combination being thought likely to reduce development, procurement and operating costs. Powered by a pair of advanced turbofan engines, the F-111 has a speed well in excess of Mach 2, and proved itself capable of undertaking the strike, attack and reconnaissance roles previously performed by a number of different types.

In many respects the F-111 lived up to expectations from the beginning of the programme, but rising costs, engine limitations and airframe weight all caused problems. Nonetheless the TFX, as the type was known before it first flew in 1964, has proved a versatile and hard-hitting aircraft, eventually meeting or exceeding most of its performance requirements in a highly successful service career intended to continue into the next century. It should be noted, however, that the F-111B naval version was cancelled at an early stage of its development due to intractable weight problems. The real virtues of the machine were initially obscured by political controversy over its cost, and worries about a basic design flaw after several early aircraft were lost for no apparent reason in the Vietnam War. A simple technical problem was then diagnosed and cured, and the F-111 matured as an exceptional combat aeroplane.

The Tupolev Tu-4, the Soviet copy of the B-29, was in service in 1947, less than two years after work on the project began. And if two years seems a long time merely to copy another aeroplane and put it into mass production, it must be remembered that the Soviet designers had to dismantle the American aircraft, produce working drawings of every component, and supervise all the modifications that had to be effected to suit the type to

The Vickers Valiant was the first of the three British 'V-bombers', and was planned as a comparatively simple type to provide Bomber Command with an interim nuclear bombing capability in the period it took to develop the two more advanced types, the Avro Vulcan with its large delta wing and the Handley Page Victor with its crescent-shaped wing. The Valiant proved successful in service and could have been developed into a successful low-level bomber of the type that began to become essential from the late 1950s as the availability of surface-to-air missile systems made high-altitude penetration of Soviet airspace increasingly problematic. The availability of the Vulcan and Valiant scotched this concept for a Valiant B.Mk 2, and the original Valiant B.Mk 1 bombers were retired in 1965 as a result of wing spar fatigue problems.

The Boeing B-52 Stratofortress was the manned bomber mainstay of the US Air Force's Strategic Air Command between the time it entered service in its initial B-52B production form during 1955 until it was complemented by the Rockwell B-1B Lancer in the later 1980s.

Soviet production techniques and methods. Metallurgists had to discover what alloys the Americans had used and instruct Soviet producers to achieve the same results; and the engineers and planners had to produce entirely new factories and techniques to build a type markedly different from any of their own. Yet the advantages were colossal: in the B-29 the Soviets found good examples of all the latest American systems, and these they could copy and modify without a long preliminary research phase.

This treasure trove was quickly exploited in the Tu-16 'Badger', the USSR's first turbojet-powered strategic bomber, which appeared in 1954 and inherited much from Tupolev's continued effort to evolve bombers, transports and even airliners from the basic Tu-4. The wings of the Tu-16 are well swept, and the two Soviet-designed engines are neatly buried in the wing roots. The Tu-16 was a match for its Western contemporaries in every

Developed in the late 1940s by English Electric, the Canberra was intended as a light tactical bomber with the ability to deliver a small nuclear weapon as an alternative to conventional free-fall weapons. The aeroplane proved immensely versatile, and was thus evolved into a number of other forms for tasks as diverse as night intruding, reconnaissance, electronic warfare and training. The type illustrated here is a Canberra T.Mk 17, which was produced in small numbers as a conversion of the Canberra B.Mk 2 bomber for the electronic warfare training role. The Canberra is still in limited first-line service with a number of smaller air forces, and also with the Royal Air Force as a trainer.

The British started to develop their own nuclear weapons in the period after World War II, and in 1946 the Royal Air Force issued an ambitious requirement for a bomber to carry such a 10,000lb (4,536kg) 'special weapon' or a heavy load of conventional bombs over a great range at high subsonic speed at an altitude of over 50,000ft (15,240m). Among the several companies who responded to this requirement were the two companies which had supplied the RAF's two most important heavy bomber types in World War II, the Avro Lancaster and the Handley Page Halifax. That from Avro was the Type 698, which was based on a circular-section fuselage that accommodated, from front to rear, the large bombing radar, pressurised flightdeck, twin-wheel nose unit of the retractable tricycle landing gear, fuel tankage, weapon bay, and bays for avionics and electronic countermeasures. The fuselage supported the large vertical tail surface and the wing centre section, which was a deep structure that carried two Bristol BE.10 (later Bristol Siddeley Olympus) turbojets on each side. Outboard of the centre section were the main panels of the delta wing, each swept at 50 degrees, accommodating one of the main landing gear units (each carrying four small twin-tired wheels) and five large fuel tanks, and carrying on their trailing edges two-section inboard elevators and two-section outboard ailerons. Two Type 698 prototypes were ordered. The first of these made its first flight in August 1952 with an interim powerplant of four Rolls-Royce Avon RA.3 turbojets each rated at 6,500lb (2,948kg) st, but these were soon replaced by Armstrong Siddeley Sapphire ASSa.6 turbojets each rated at 7,500lb (3,402kg) st and later by Olympus BOl.1/28 turbojets. The second prototype was closer to the planned production standard with its forward fuselage lengthened by 1 ft 4 in (0.406 m) to accommodate the longer nose unit leg that had been installed to provide the wing with a greater angle of incidence at take-off. The name Vulcan had by now been selected for the bomber, and the first Vulcan B.Mk 1 to emerge from the production line flew in February 1955 with the Olympus Mk 100 turbojet that was soon replaced by quartets of steadily more powerful Olympus variants. Production totalled 45 aircraft that entered service from February 1957.

respect, and more than a match in defensive armament.

Tupolev sprang a further surprise on the aviation world in 1955, with the very large Tu-95 'Bear' bomber. Powered by four 14,795hp (10,030kW) Kuznetsov turboprop engines driving very large contra-rotating propeller units, the Tu-95 was sleek and the wings were moderately swept. The type had an excellent range of 7,457 miles (12,000km) and a maximum speed in the order of 559mph (900km/h).

Both the Tu-16 and Tu-95 remain in service with the Russian air force, the former usually employed in roles such as maritime reconnaissance, missile launching and air-to-air tanking, and the latter in longer-range

Generally known in the West as the 'Badger', the Tupolev Tu-16 strategic medium bomber was a remarkable type for the time of its design and development in the late 1940s and early 1950s, achieving considerable payload/range performance with two notably powerful turbojet engines. Built in substantial numbers, the Tu-16 was initially used in the level bombing role, but was then adapted in considerable numbers for other tasks such as inflight refuelling, launch of large nuclear-tipped missiles, multi-sensor reconnaissance, and electronic warfare. The type is still in useful service, but is finally being phased out of first-line service.

The Mikoyan-Gurevich MiG-23 'Flogger' was designed as an air-combat fighter to succeed the MiG-21 'Fishbed', and was most notably different from its predecessor not only in its greater size, weight, power and electronic sophistication, but also in its adoption of a variable-geometry wing planform in which the minimum-sweep position provided good take-off and landing performance. The medium-sweep position provided a good blend of speed and range, and the maximum-sweep position provided the highest possible performance. This variant is a MiG-23MF 'Flogger-B', which was the first large-scale production model.

maritime reconnaissance, missile launching and strategic bombing. A modernised variant of the TU-95 was evolved as the Tu-142, which is used for the long-range anti-submarine role.

The other important heavy bomber developed by the Soviets in the 1950s was the Myasishchyev M-4 'Bison', which entered service in 1958. Like the Boeing bombers, it perched on a tandem main landing gear arrangement with outrigger units for ground stability. Finally removed from service in the late 1980s, the M-4 was powered by four turbojets buried in the wing roots, but while it was nearly as large as the B-52, the M-4 could carry only a 22,046lb (10,000kg) weapon load, and both its speed and range were inferior to that of its American counterpart. The Soviets judged early in the type's career that the M-4 was operationally inferior to the Tu-95, despite the latter's reliance on a turboprop powerplant, and the M-4 was switched to the shorter-range strategic role before being converted as an air-to-air tanker.

To match the B-58 supersonic bomber, the Soviets revealed the existence of the Tu-22 'Blinder' in 1961. This is another sleek aeroplane of aggressive but somewhat unusual appearance as its two engines are located above the tailplane, one on each side of the vertical tail surfaces. The Tu-22, which also came as a shock to the West, is capable of Mach 1.5 but was considered deficient in range by the Soviets.

These aircraft were kept in the forefront of Soviet bomber capability for as long as possible by updating their electronics and improving their engines. The aircraft were adapted for carrying more advanced weapons, including stand-off missiles, but they grew in obsolescence during the mid-1960s, and many were converted for the maritime reconnaissance role, as their economical cruising range was more important than outright speed or weapon-carrying capability.

The USSR's next strategic bomber was a formidable aircraft, the variable-geometry Tu-22M 'Backfire'. Capable of Mach 2.3 at high altitude, the 'Backfire' can carry the largest free-fall nuclear weapons or a pair of stand-off missiles.

The Americans did not continue with the concept of supersonic medium bombers after the B-58, but decided instead designed a supersonic heavy

The Tupolev Tu-95 was one of two swept-wing strategic bombers developed in the USSR from the late 1940s, initially as a back-up in the event of problems with the conceptually more advanced Myasishchyev M-4 'Bison' with turbojet propulsion. The Tu-95 resulted from a 1950 initial decision to design and develop a technically less risky bomber that could fill the operational gap that would be left should the M-4 prove unsuccessful, and was based on the extraordinarily powerful NK-12 turboprop. The engine and its contra-rotating propeller unit were a great technical risk, but in structural terms the Tu-95 was not, for it was derived ultimately from the Tu-4. The Tu-95/1 first of two proto-types flew in September 1955 and revealed generally satisfactory performance and handling even though there were severe engine/propeller problems that were probably responsible for the loss of this aeroplane. The Tu-95/2 second prototype followed the Tu-95/1 into the air in February 1955. With the engine/propeller problems reduced – though not eliminated – the new bomber entered service early in 1956 as the Tu-95M that soon received the NATO reporting name 'Bear-A'.

bomber for the penetration role. This aeroplane was the Rockwell B-1, which offered excellent capabilities in a role that became obsolete in the face of a steadily improved Soviet surface-to-air missile capability. The B-1 project was therefore cancelled in its high-supersonic B-1A form, only to be reinstated later as the more modestly supersonic B-1B Lancer, optimised for the low-level role. As an alternative to the B-1A, the Americans decided to procure more ballistic missiles (both submarine- and land-launched) and large numbers of the new generation of cruise missiles. These small turbofan-powered 'aircraft' carry a potent warhead, and are guided by an inertial navigation system (INS) that is updated over major landmarks by

Light bombers have been in decline since the end of World War II, principally because attack fighters can pack almost as great a punch and are considerably cheaper to build and operate. There have been two classic examples: the British-built English Electric Canberra, and the Soviet Ilyushin Il-28 'Beagle'. The Canberra was conceived in 1945, and the first prototype flew in 1949. Since then the aircraft has served with great distinction in many air forces, including that of the United States, and still has a limited future in smaller air forces. Extremely versatile and manoeuvrable, the Canberra could outfly most of the fighters of its heyday, and established a number of records. The Il-28 flew two years before the British bomber, and despite its obsolescence is still a popular aeroplane in the countries within the former Soviet sphere of influence.

The Americans have not relied on conversions of bombers for their maritime reconnaissance aircraft, but have produced such excellent machines as the Lockheed P2V Neptune, and the Lockheed (now Lockheed Martin) P-3 Orion, derived from the Electra airliner. After years of service from the Avro Shackleton derivative of the Lincoln, the RAF currently deploys the four-engined Hawker Siddeley Nimrod, based very loosely on the Comet airliner. This is possibly the best maritime reconnaissance aeroplane in the world, and combines long endurance on two engines with a high-speed dash capability when using all four. The Nimrod is the only such aeroplane in the world powered by turbojets rather than turboprops. Several other countries have also produced useful maritime reconnaissance

The Saab 35 Draken was the first genuinely supersonic warplane of Western European design to enter production, and was a remarkable achievement for the small Swedish aircraft industry as the Draken offered basically the same performance as the English Electric Lightning with only half the power (one rather than two Rolls-Royce Avon turbojets fitted in this instance with a Swedish-designed afterburner). The key to this remarkable performance was the creation of a long aeroplane with most of the major masses piled one behind the other, resulting in an aeroplane of very small frontal area supported in the air by a 'double-delta' wing whose highly swept inboard sections were little more than the inlet ducts for the turbojet engine installed in the rear fuselage.

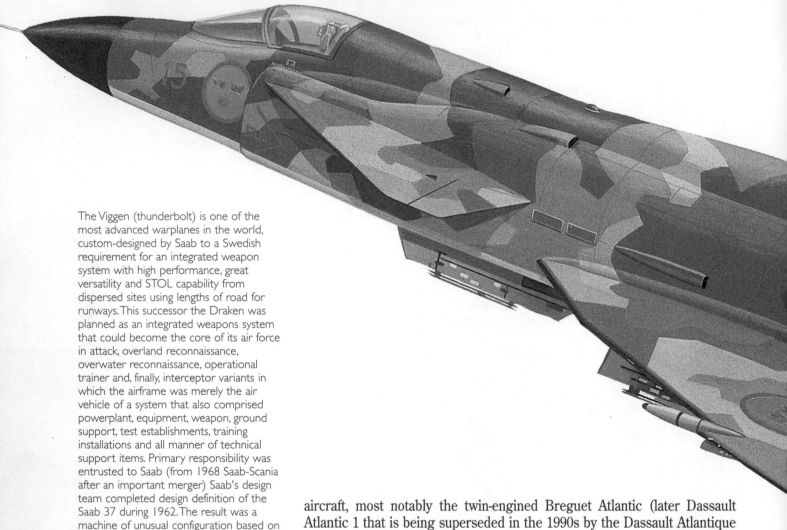

The Viggen (thunderbolt) is one of the most advanced warplanes in the world, custom-designed by Saab to a Swedish requirement for an integrated weapon system with high performance, great versatility and STOL capability from dispersed sites using lengths of road for runways. This successor the Draken was planned as an integrated weapons system that could become the core of its air force in attack, overland reconnaissance, overwater reconnaissance, operational trainer and, finally, interceptor variants in which the airframe was merely the air vehicle of a system that also comprised powerplant, equipment, weapon, ground support, test establishments, training installations and all manner of technical support items. Primary responsibility was entrusted to Saab (from 1968 Saab-Scania after an important merger) Saab's design team completed design definition of the Saab 37 during 1962. The result was a machine of unusual configuration based on a large double-delta wing, though this reversed the planform of the Draken's wing in having greater sweep outboard than inboard. This was only the start of the story, however, as the need for real STOL capability drove the rest of the basic design in a direction that was for its time most radical. Thus the double-delta wing was located at the rear of the fuselage in the low-set position, and complemented by canard foreplanes set in the shoulder position on the inlet trunks just to the rear of the cockpit. Whereas the conventional delta-winged warplane must use up-elevon to raise the nose for take-off, thereby imposing an overall download, the canard delta-winged warplane employs the lift of the canard foreplane halves to raise the nose, thereby creating an overall upload for highly beneficial effects on take-off run.

aircraft, most notably the twin-engined Breguet Atlantic (later Dassault Atlantic 1 that is being superseded in the 1990s by the Dassault Atlantique 2) landplane from France, the four-engined ShinMaywa (originally Shin Meiwa) PS-1 flying boat from Japan, and the four-engined Ilyushin Il-38 'May' landplane from the USSR.

The only other country to have produced advanced combat aircraft is Sweden, whose policy of strongly armed neutrality led to the development of the highly original and very interesting Saab 35 Draken (dragon) double-delta and Saab 37 Viggen (thunderbolt) canard multi-role aircraft, both capable of performance in the region of Mach 2. The success of these two Swedish aircraft should have been an object lesson for the West: the authorities decided what they needed, and then every effort was made to develop the right machine for the specification. Although costly, such a programme never approached the vastly expensive competitive programmes initiated in other countries.

The vast cost of advanced aircraft determined that aircraft produced by other nations have been of limited performance. In the 1960's, even the rich European countries reached the stage where collaborative projects became both financially and politically attractive: only in this way could the costs be spread to a sufficient number of taxpayers, and large, relatively economical production runs assured. Excellent examples of the trend were the SEPECAT strike, attack and reconnaissance fighter built by the United Kingdom and France, the Panavia Tornado variable-geometry multi-role combat aeroplane built by the United Kingdom, West Germany and Italy,

Developed by McDonnell Douglas in association with British Aerospace, which includes the Hawker company that developed the original Harrier, the AV-8B Harrier II is a considerably more advanced warplane that the Harrier with an uprated engine, a revised cockpit offering better fields of vision and more advanced instrumentation, a larger and more sophisticated wing of all-composite construction, superior lift-improvement devices, and provision for a somewhat larger load of more diverse and capable weapon types. These basic changes are complemented by a more advanced nav/attack system that has been complemented in later subvariants by a forward-looking infra-red sensor for passive night-attack capability, and radar for full all-weather capability.

About to enter a mid-life upgrade programme in the later 1990s, the Panavia Tornado is a collaborative British, German and Italian type optimised for the long-range interdiction role but also developed in air-superiority and electronic warfare/reconnaissance variants for the British and the Germans and Italian respectively. The Tornado IDS baseline variant illustrated here can carry a heavy external weapons load, possesses STOL capability as a result of its high-lift devices and thrust-reversing engines, can cruise over long ranges with its variable-geometry wing in the minimum- or intermediate-sweep positions, can fly very fast at very low level with its wings in the maximum-sweep position, and can undertake blind first-pass attacks with very considerable accuracy with its advanced avionics, which include terrain-following radar and an inertial navigation system.

and the Dassault/Dornier Alpha Jet light attack/trainer aeroplane built by France and West Germany. Such co-operation was financially reasonable for the countries concerned and gave opportunities for the creation of exciting new aircraft.

The Hawker Siddeley (now British Aerospace) Harrier vertical take-off and landing (VTOL) aeroplane, with its radical arrangement of vectoring jetpipes to deflect the engine's thrust, was one of the last major combat aircraft to be built by a single nation, along with examples from the United States, Russia, France, China and Sweden.

During the first half of the 1980s, the United Kingdom was actively seeking partners for the collaborative development of the Agile Combat Aircraft technology demonstrator, to be built as a vital step towards the evolution of a new European combat aircraft based on the British Aerospace P.110 design, with contributions from West German and French companies: this effort finally matured as the Eurofighter 2000. The Harrier concept crossed the Atlantic to the United States, where McDonnell Douglas was largely responsible for the much enhanced AV-8B Harrier II for the US Marine Corps and, in British-assembled form, the Harrier GR.Mk 5 for the RAF.

In the field of combat aircraft capability, the features being developed in the 1980s were not performance factors as such, but were consentrated on improved combat capability through aspects such as increased agility, weapons flexibility, accuracy of navigation and weapons delivery, and operational reliability. Advances were thus being made in the sphere of avionics and the control of aircraft in all flight regimes by the use of electronically signalled control movements ('fly-by-wire' control system), advanced aerodynamics and engines with considerably improved power-to-weight ratios.

This led to a new generation of combat aircraft, epitomised by production machines such as the General Dynamics F-16 Fighting Falcon and McDonnell Douglas F/A-18 Hornet, and planned developments such as the ACA, a re-winged version of the F-16 evaluated as the F-16XL, and the Saab JAS 39 Gripen (griffon) fighter. Much was also being achieved in the enhancement of existing capabilities, exemplified by the provision of canard foreplanes on the Dassault Mirage 4000 prototype and the Israel Aircraft Industries Kfir-C2 production fighter, and by the increasing use of improved targeting aids carried as external pods.

Through the Present Into the Future

THE manned aeroplane is here to stay for the foreseeable future. During the period from the late 1950's to the early 1970s, there were hints that the manned warplane would soon be replaced by guided missiles, but this evolution has not taken place for a number of pressing technical reasons and because of the importance of an onboard crew to the operational versatility and flexibility of the warplane.

The importance of human intervention is nowhere better attested than in the control of the strategic nuclear deterrents of the two superpowers up to the time of the USSR's collapse in 1989. The USA and USSR each had large numbers of surface- and underwater-launched ballistic missiles, but they retained comparatively small but significant manned bomber forces that could be re-targeted after 'launch', could be recalled, could undertake a variety of approaches to the target, and could fly other missions with the aid of additional or different equipment.

The Soviets' most important such assets, which are still operated by some of the USSR's successor states in the Commonwealth of Independent States (CIS), such as Russia and the Ukraine, are the Tupolev Tu-22M 'Backfire' and the Tu-160 'Blackjack' variable-geometry bombers. The Tu-22M is a radical development of the disappointing Tu-22 'Blinder' fixed-wing bomber, while the TU-160 bears a striking likeness to the Rockwell B-1 Lancer, the American type designed as successor to the Boeing B-52 Stratofortress. The B-52 was designed for long-range subsonic missions, carrying free-fall nuclear weapons, but in its last B-52G and B-52H variants it was revised for ow-level penetration of Soviet airspace, armed with two North American AGM-28 Hound Dog air-to-surface supersonic cruise missiles later replaced by 12 or more Boeing AGM-86 air-to-surface subsonic cruise missiles. As a result of its extreme targeting accuracy and relative immunity to interception due to its very low-level

—— Lockheed Martin F-16 Fighting Falcon ——

THIS illustration shows the original F-16A with a number of its weapon options. The current F-16C differs externally only in a number of minor features such as a larger tailplane, but has the option of two considerably more powerful engines as well as a much improved suite of flight and mission avionics for a considerably improved as well as expanded capability. The primary details of the F-16C, whose pilot sits on a semi-reclining McDonnell Douglas ACES II zero/zero ejector seat and controls the fighter with his right-hand sidestick controller and left-hand throttle, include a powerplant of one General Electric F110-GE-129 or Pratt & Whitney F100-P-229 turbofan rated respectively at 29,588 or 29,100lb (13,421 or 13,200kg) st with afterburning, span of 32ft 9.75in (32.00m) including wing-tip missiles, length of 49ft 4in (15.03m), maximum take-off weight of 42,300lb (19,187kg), maximum speed of more than 1,320mph (2,124km/h) or Mach 2.0 at high altitude, service ceiling of more than 50,000ft (15,240m), tactical radius of 852 miles (1,371km) with two 2,000lb (907kg) bombs and two AIM-9 Sidewinder air-to-air missiles, and an armament of one 20 mm M61A1 Vulcan six-barrel cannon and up to 12,000lb (5,443kg) of stores carried on nine hardpoints.

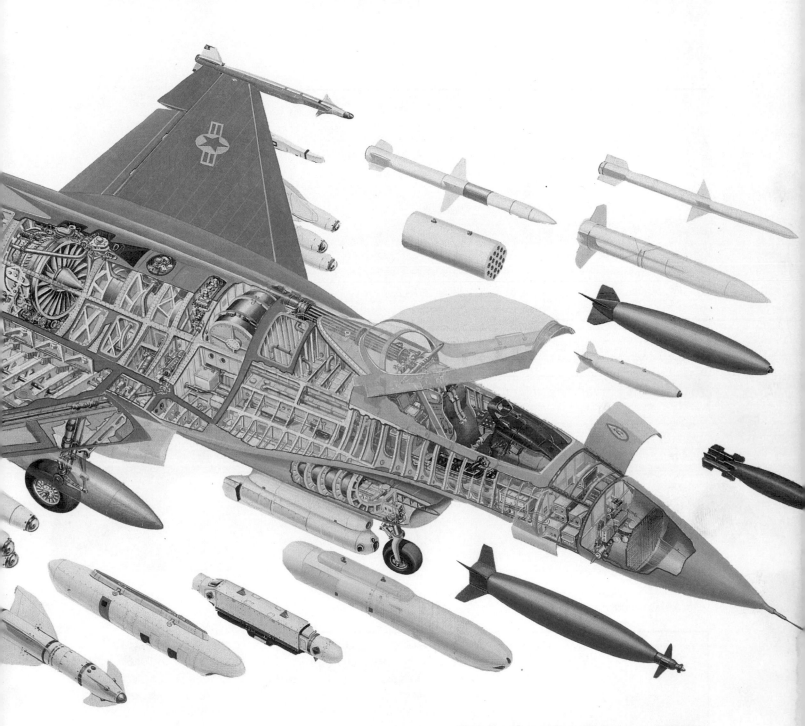

Originally a General Dynamics but now a Lockheed Martin product, the F-16 Fighting Falcon was developed initially as a light-weight fighter technology demonstrator with a fly-by-wire control system and an airframe of relaxed static stability, the combination of the two offering a level of agility considerably higher than that of machines such as the McDonnell Douglas F-4 Phantom II. So successful were the YF-16 prototypes, however, that the type was ordered into production and has since been developed into a superb multi-role fighter.

This trio of Lockheed (now Lockheed Martin) S-3 carrierborne anti-submarine aircraft reveals a number of interesting features. The aeroplane nearest the camera shows the magnetic anomaly detector 'sting' in the extended position for the detection of a submerged submarine by the localised effect of its large ferrous mass on the Earth's magnetic field, and the aeroplane farthest from the camera is a KS-3A inflight-refuelling tanker conversion with its drogue-tipped hose in the trailed position so that a receiver aeroplane can manoeuvre its refuelling probe into the drogue and take on fuel.

cruise altitude and 'stealthy' design, the AGM-86 offered far higher penetration capability than the AGM-28.

The B-1A was designed for high supersonic performance at high altitude, but the growing sophistication of the Soviet air-defence capability led to the type's cancellation, although it was later reinstated as the B-1B with lower overall performance, but with superior capabilities in the penetration role achieved through a large complement of cruise missiles and/or free-fall nuclear weapons. In simple financial terms, it is hard to appreciate how the B-1B programme could be justified as truly cost-effective, but in strategic and political terms there can be no doubt that the type provides the United States with important capabilities in the power-projection role, which demands extreme operational flexibility up to the moment of weapon release.

The B-1B is an exceptional illustration, inasmuch as the cost and complexity of a single-role aeroplane makes such types rare in modern air forces, where single-role aircraft are generally dedicated either to specialised reconnaissance – as exemplified by the Lockheed (now Lockheed Martin) SR-71 and the TR-1 updated version of the classic U-2 in

Concerned that a planned Super Mirage (Mirage IIIG8A with a powerplant of two SNECMA M53-3 turbofans) for the Avion de Combat Futur requirement would prove too costly for the French air force, Dassault offered the service a smaller multi-role fighter with a delta wing and single engine, this design having been prepared in 1972 as the Delta 1000. During 1975 the French air force belatedly reached the same conclusion as Dassault about the cost of the Super Mirage program, and in December of that year cancelled the ACF requirement in favour of four prototypes (complemented by a company-funded fifth machine) of the delta-winged type in a revised form dubbed Mirage 2000. Dassault was wrongly convinced that the Mirage 2000 would be much cheaper to develop and build than the Super Mirage, but was correct in anticipating that the use of the latest CCV (Control-Configured Vehicle) concepts in concert with advanced technology would make the Mirage 2000 into a warplane offering capabilities enormously superior to those of the Mirage III with basically the same layout. The core of this superior capability was the combination of relaxed static stability, an area-ruled fuselage, a cambered wing carrying automatically scheduled full-span slats on its leading edges and full-span elevons on its trailing edges, and a fly-by-wire control system. The first prototype flew in March 1978, and the type entered service in July 1984 as the Mirage 2000C fighter. The type has since been developed in a number of single- and two-seat variants for a host of roles.

American service, or the Myasishchyev M-17/55 'Mystic' entering Russian service in the mid-1990s – or to control as exemplified by the Boeing E-3A Sentry, developed from the Model 707 transport, and the Ilyushin A-50 'Mainstay' developed from the Il-76 'Candid' transport. These extremely costly aircraft have good survival chances as they are not intended for operations in the combat zone.

The SR-71 'Blackbird' was retired from first-line service in the early 1990s, but is still in limited use for experimental tasks, and a few aircraft were restored to operational capability in 1995. The SR-71 is a truly remarkable aeroplane, and remains the current holder of the world's absolute speed and altitude records. Its origins are still veiled, but it is clear that the type was planned as the launch platform for supersonic reconnaissance drones, developed initially into the YF-12A experimental interceptor and later into the SR-71 strategic reconnaissance platform. The 'Blackbird' is a massive delta-wing machine with the fuselage contours faired laterally into a lifting shape, and is powered by two afterburning bleed-turbojets running on special low-volatility fuel. Prodigiously expensive to build and to maintain, the SR-71 fleet provided the US forces with a mass of reconnaissance information after Mach 3+ flights at exceptionally high altitudes.

For the control of its armed forces, the United States deploys two types modified from civil airliners. As noted above, the Boeing E-3 Sentry is an adaptation of the Boeing 707, with a large rotodome above the fuselage containing the antenna for the very capable Westinghouse APY-1 radar. Operating at high altitude on long patrols, the E-3 can monitor all air activity within a radius of 250 miles (402km) at any altitude, while an onboard tactical team uses computers to assess data from this radar and other sources, and then directs friendly forces to deal with the threats revealed. The United States planned a fleet of 40 Sentries but in fact ordered just 34 aircraft, while later purchasers were NATO with 18, Saudi Arabia with five, France with four and the United Kingdom with seven. The USSR's first such aeroplane was the considerably less sophisticated Tupolev Tu-126 'Moss', replaced early in the 1990's by the A-50 'Mainstay' derivative of the Il-76 'Candid' transport.

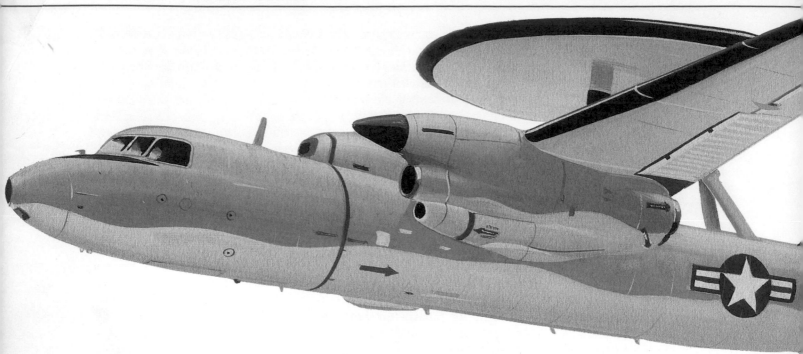

These airborne warning and control system aircraft (AWACS) are exceedingly complex yet efficient adjuncts to the tactical control of air power: essentially, they are airborne command posts, generating data for themselves and receiving inputs from other aircraft, satellites and surface forces. Each aeroplane is capable of controlling the entire range of air activities in a complete theatre of war.

The control of tactical air operations has also become increasingly important, and the world's most successful exponent of this art is the Grumman (now Northrop Grumman) E-2 Hawkeye, which was developed for carrierborne use by the US Navy and has proved itself particularly effective, notably during the Israeli invasion of Lebanon in early 1982. The E-2 was still in production during the mid-1990s for the US Navy, which had ordered almost 200 such aircraft by that time, and other purchasers include Egypt, France, Israel, Japan, Singapore and Taiwan.

Although expensive, this type of aeroplane can increase the efficiency of combat aircraft, hence the description of such aircraft as 'force multipliers'. It is probable, therefore, that AWACS aircraft are likely to figure prominently in the future plans of the major air forces. However, just as it is desirable to make full use of one's own AWACS aircraft, it is equally important to prevent the enemy from making full use of his. It seems likely, therefore, that the role of electronic counter-measures (ECM) aircraft will be extended from

Below: Better known in the West as the 'Flogger', the Mikoyan-Gurevich MiG-23 was developed as successor to the MiG-21 'Fishbed', and was better optimised for the tactical situation that developed from the later 1960s in being a larger and more comprehensively equipped (and also armed) type with a considerably more powerful engine and, perhaps most importantly of all, a variable-geometry wing planform in which the minimum-sweep position offered good field performance, the intermediate-sweep position provided good cruise performance, and the maximum-sweep position helped to generate high overall performance at the upper end of the speed range. The type was extensively developed up to the late 1980s as the MiG-23 for the fighter and to a limited extent fighter-bomber roles, and as the somewhat modified MiG-27 for the dedicated attack role with an armoured forward fuselage, and greater weapon capability.

The Grumman E-2 Hawkeye is a remarkable carrierborne aeroplane offering an AWACS (Airborne Warning And Control System) capability in no way inferior in qualitative terms to that of the larger, land-based Boeing E-3 Sentry. The features that have been sacrificed to secure the capability for operations from the flightdecks of the US Navy's aircraft carriers are airframe size and engine power, and this means that the E-2 has a lower speed and shorter endurance than the E-3, although both of these elements are adequate for naval operations.

its already prominent position. The US Air Force pioneered the use of such aircraft over Vietnam in the 1960s and early 1970s, and they have proved themselves valuable aids to combat aircraft, jamming the radar of enemy ground and air missiles and hampering the use of early warning systems.

The deployment of electronic warfare aircraft increased considerably during the 1980s, primarily in the USA. Few countries can afford to purchase single-role aircraft such as the US Navy's Grumman (now Northrop Grumman) EA-6 Prowler all-weather type, which has capabilities at strategic, operational and tactical levels, and therefore rely on the extensive use of podded ECM equipment located on underwing hardpoints otherwise dedicated to the carriage of weapon and/or drop tanks. There is little doubt, however, that the increased survivability of combat aircraft carrying ECM pods more than offsets their reduced disposable warload. ECM pods are standard on the combat aircraft of all air forces with any claim to modern equipment.

Two other AEW aircraft worthy of mention are the Grumman (now Northrop Grumman) EF-111 Raven (or 'Electric Fox'), of which 42 were produced for the US Air Force as conversions of obsolescent General Dynamics F-111A long-range interdictors but with a highly automated version of the same Raytheon ALQ-99 Tactical Jamming System as carried by the EA-6 Prowler; and the Panavia Tornado ECR development of the Tornado multi-role warplane for electronic combat and reconnaissance roles, which include the detection and elimination of radars associated with enemy air-defence systems.

The United States, the former USSr, and Western European nations have introduced new combat aircraft in recent years. The most important of these are: the Mikoyan-Gurevich MiG-23 'Flogger' variable-geometry tactical fighter, the MiG-27 'Flogger' attack fighter derivative of the MiG-23, the Sukhoi Su-24 'Fencer' variable-geometry strike and attack aeroplane, and the Su-25 'Frogfoot' close-support and anti-tank aeroplane for the Warsaw Pact forces; the Fairchild Republic A-10 Thunderbolt II anti-tank aeroplane, the General Dynamics F-16 Fighting Falcon air-combat and multi-role fighter, the Grumman (now Northrop Grumman) F-14 Tomcat carrierborne multi-role fighter with a variable-geometry wing platform, the McDonnell Douglas F-15 Eagle air-superiority fighter, and the McDonnell Douglas/Northrop F/A-18 Hornet carrierborne dual-role fighter/attack aeroplane for the United States; the Dassault-Breguet Mirage F1 and Mirage 2000 for France; and the variable-geometry Panavia Tornado multi-role combat aeroplane for Italy, the United Kingdom and Germany.

Although most of these are large, expensive combat aircraft, the American F-16 and F/A-18 are lighter aircraft designed to cope with the

The McDonnell Douglas F-15 Eagle is the air-superiority counterpart of the Lockheed Martin F-16 Fighting Falcon air-combat fighter, and like its smaller colleague has been developed into a true multi-role type able to carry a heavy load of diverse 'smart' and 'dumb' air-to-surface weapons as an alternative to its primary load of short- and medium-range air-to-air missiles. The F-15 was planned as successor to the McDonnell Douglas F-4 Phantom II in its Sidewinder and Sparrow missile-armed form, and possesses a core similarity to the earlier type in its substantial twin-engined airframe with a large wing for considerable internal fuel capacity and a high rate of climb to a considerable service ceiling.

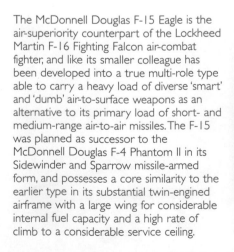

125

Above: Originally known as the U-2 and then as the TR-1 before returning to U-1 once more, this Lockheed Martin type is essentially a jet-powered 'glider' able to operate at very high altitudes in the reconnaissance role.

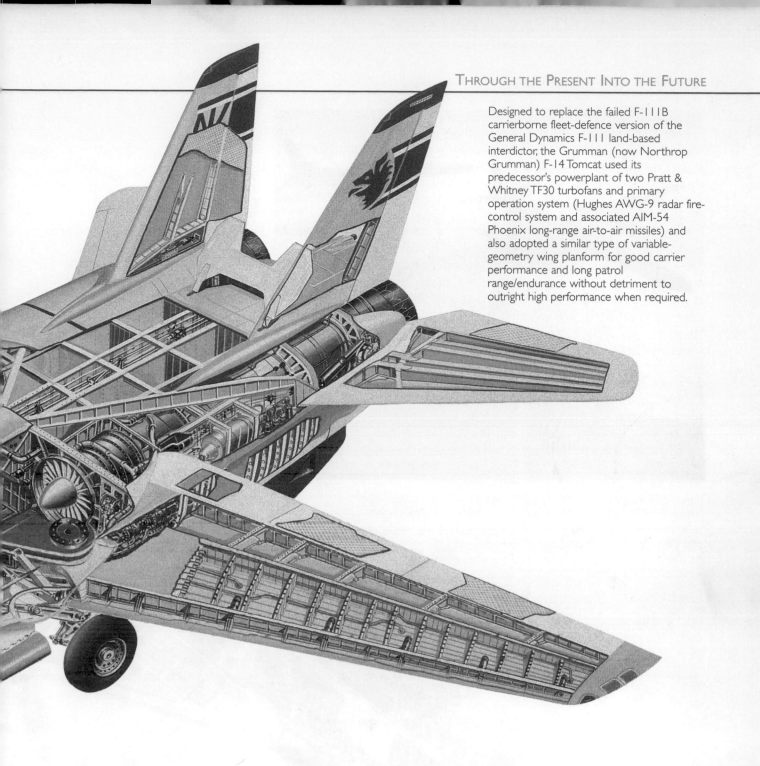

Designed to replace the failed F-111B carrierborne fleet-defence version of the General Dynamics F-111 land-based interdictor, the Grumman (now Northrop Grumman) F-14 Tomcat used its predecessor's powerplant of two Pratt & Whitney TF30 turbofans and primary operation system (Hughes AWG-9 radar fire-control system and associated AIM-54 Phoenix long-range air-to-air missiles) and also adopted a similar type of variable-geometry wing planform for good carrier performance and long patrol range/endurance without detriment to outright high performance when required.

Northrop Grumman F-14 Tomcat

CERTAINLY the most powerfully armed carrierborne fighter in the world and, despite its age, still one of the most capable air-superiority fighters of any type anywhere in the world, the F-14 Tomcat (seen here in its original F-14A version before development of the F-14D version with a different powerplant) is a high-performance platform for carriage of the AWG-9 radar system and AIM-54 Phoenix long-range AAM, of which a maximum of six can be carried, reduced to four if the underwing hardpoints are used for four AIM-9 Sidewinder short-range AAMs or alternatively for two AIM-9s and two AIM-7 Sparrow medium-range AAMs, which can also replace the AIM-54s on the underfuselage stations; there is also a 20 mm M61A1 Vulcan six-barrel cannon for dogfighting engagements. The F-14A has a crew of two (pilot and systems operator) in tandem on Martin-Baker GRU7A zero/zero ejector seats, a powerplant of two Pratt & Whitney TF-30-P-414A turbofans each rated at 20,900lb (9,480kg) st with afterburning, span of 64ft 1.5in (19.55m) spread reducing to 38 ft 2.5in (11.65m) swept, length of 62ft 8in (19.10m), empty weight of 40,104 lb (18,191kg), maximum take-off weight of 74,349 lb (33724 kg), maximum speed of 1,564mph (2,517km/h) or Mach 2.27 at 36,000ft (10,975m), initial climb rate of more than 30,000 ft (9145 m) per minute, service ceiling of more than 56,000ft (17,070m), and range of 2,000 miles (3,220km) in interceptor configuration with drop tanks.

attentions of heavier and more sophisticated combat aircraft through their extraordinary agility and the sophisticated electronics. In Europe, this tendency is illustrated in the later Dassault fighters and the SEPECAT Jaguar strike fighter. The move towards variable-geometry layouts combines economy and low landing speed with high combat speed, while new alloys and materials such as carbon-fibre and high-strength plastics are also being introduced.

At a purely tactical level, the tendency away from Mach 2+ performance towards much reduced performance is best exemplified by the A-10 Thunderbolt II, which is a twin-engined type intended for the battlefield anti-tank and close-support roles. Almost ugly in appearance, the A-10 has a combination of exceptional strength and complete redundancy of principal systems, providing a high level of battlefield survivability. Comparatively cheap to buy, operate and maintain, the A-10 performs well in terms of endurance and agility at low altitudes with a large payload, and is capable of delivering heavy offensive loads of free-fall or precision-guided weapons very accurately in the face of intense anti-aircraft fire. Other nations have already experimented with this type of machine, but usually in the form of a counter-insurgency aircraft based on light aircraft or primary trainers. The Soviet (now Russian) equivalent to the A-10 is the Sukhoi Su-25 'Frogfoot', which was revealed to be in limited service over Afghanistan in 1982, and has since been developed both into a carrierborne and a land-based attack fighter, offering offensive capabilities

The McDonnell Douglas F-15 Eagle is a thoroughbred fighter with much in common with the same company's F-4 Phantom II at the conceptual level in features such as the large and only modestly swept wing, and the boomed carriage of the tail unit: on this F-4 this is a single unit above the twin-engined powerplant, but on the F-15 it comprises paired units outside the twin-engined powerplant.

McDonnell Douglas F-15 Eagle

THE McDonnell Douglas F-15 Eagle air-superiority fighter is a large and highly capable type offering multi-role as well as interception capabilities, and is notable for its ability to carry CFTs (Conformal Fuel Tanks) on the outsides of its inlet trunks for considerably more fuel and tangential weapon-carriage capability. The single-seat variants are the baseline F-15A with APG-63 radar and a powerplant of two Pratt & Whitney F100-P-100 turbofans each rated at 23,380lb (10,809kg) with afterburning, and the F-15C with significantly enhanced APG-70 radar and an uprated powerplant. The two-seat models are the combat-capable F-15B and F-15D equivalent to the F-15A and F-15C respectively, and the F-15E long-range interdictor with CFTs and much enhanced weapons capability. The F-15C is powered by two Pratt & Whitney F100-P-220 turbofans each rated at 23,450lb (10,637kg) st with afterburning. The fighter's other data include a span of 42ft 9.75in (13.05m), length of 63ft 9in (19.43m), maximum take-off weight of 68,000lb (30,844kg), maximum speed of more than 1,650mph (2,655km/h) or Mach 2.5 at 36,000ft (10,975m), initial climb rate of more than 50,000ft (15,240m) per minute, service ceiling of 60,000ft (18,290m), and tactical range of 1,222 miles (1,967km) in the interception role. The F-15C is armed with one 20 mm M61A1 Vulcan six-barrel cannon and can carry 23,600lb (10,705kg) of external stores on nine hardpoints.

comparable with those of the A-10 in addition to slightly higher performance. By the end of the 1980s the US Air Force had decided that the A-10 was obsolescent, and planned to adopt a derivative of the F-16 as its close air support/battlefield air interdiction (CAS/BAI) type. This plan was proceeding in the mid-1990s despite the fact that the A-10 proved itself a truly formidable aeroplane in intended role during the 1991 UN-led campaign to liberate Kuwait. Indeed, the success of the A-10, attracted considerable interest from countries looking to purchase second-hand aircraft.

Another type that had proved its military attractions, but yet failed to secure the success it really deserves is the VTOL aeroplane exemplified by the British Aerospace Harrier. Modern airfields, with their large expanses of runway and taxiway, are very vulnerable to the type of air and/or missile attack that can render them unusable even if they are not actually destroyed, and this poses enormous practical problems for the continued viability of conventional air power. The VTOL aeroplane is immune to this limitation, as it can operat from just behind the front line of even a highly mobile campaign.

The original Harrier was supplanted during the late 1980s and early 1990s by the Harrier II, developed jointly by McDonnell Douglas and British Aerospace for service with the US Marine Corps and RAF as the AV-8B and Harrier GR.Mk 5 respectively. The Harrier II is altogether superior to the original model in most operational aspects, as a result of its larger yet lighter wing, improved cockpit, greater load-carrying capability, more powerful engine and enhanced lift-improvement devices. Continued development has produced the Night-Attack Harrier with provision for the sensors that make possible an electronically silent night attack, and the radar-equipped Harrier II Plus which is under final development in the mid-1990s.

The only derivative of the original Harrier to remain in service in the mid-1990s is the British Aerospace Sea Harrier, which was evolved towards the end of the 1970s to provide the FAA with a radar-carrying multi-role fighter, reconnaissance and strike (attack) aeroplane able to operate from the three small Royal Navy aircraft-carriers. The type was rushed into service in time to play a highly distinguished role in the 1982 recapture of the Falklands Islands from Argentine occupation. The original Sea Harrier FRS.Mk 1 is being supplemented by the Sea Harrier F/A.Mk 2 (previously FRS.Mk 2), with superior radar and the ability to carry a larger load of more advanced weapons.

An Anglo-French collaborative programme, the SEPECAT Jaguar was planned as a supersonic advanced trainer, but proved so successful that most production aircraft were completed in single-seat attack form. The type has STOL field performance, the stalky landing gear provides good ground clearance for the loading of bulky external stores, and the availability of a high-grade nav/attack system (without radar) provides for blind first-pass attack capability.

With a larger wing and more powerful engine than the BAe (originally Hawker Siddeley) Harrier, the McDonnell Douglas/BAe AV-8 Harrier II STOVL (Short Take-Off and Vertical Landing) warplane offers a significantly improved weapon-carriage capability, and had been adopted by Italy and Spain in addition to the USA and UK.

Seen here in the form of the first of two YA-10A prototypes, the Fairchild Republic A-10A Thunderbolt II is a dedicated tank-killing and close support warplane with great strength, large quantities of armour, redundant structures and systems, and a twin-engined powerplant provided with enhanced survivability by the wide separation of the two engines and the shielding against ground fire offered by the wing and tail. The primary armament is one 30 mm GAU-8/A Avenger seven-barrel cannon firing depleted uranium projectiles, and up to 16,000 lb (7528 kg) of disposable stores (including up to six Hughes AGM-65 Maverick air-to-surface missiles) carried on 11 hardpoints.

The United States and the United Kingdom are collaborating in a project for a supersonic short take-off, vertical landing (STVOL) combat aeroplane; the only other contender in this major but wholly underestimated field has been the former USSR, where the VTOL/STOVL development is the work of the Yakovlev design bureau, whose first operational aeroplane of this type was the Yak-38 'Forger' carrierborne attack aircraft. The bureau designed the Yak-141 'Freehand' as a supersonic successor, but a number of crashes and an acute shortage of funding led to the cancellation of this programme.

The performance plateau reached with current military aircraft results from reliance on aluminium alloys as the primary structural medium, and this precludes sustained speeds in excess of Mach 2.25. Titanium is used in cases where heat is likely to be extreme, but the cost of this metal prohibits its use on a large scale. Composite materials of various kinds became more common during the 1980s, but their costs were also high and their applications somewhat specialised. Later in the decade, however, continued development of aeronautical materials made feasible the greater use of composite materials for load-carrying structures and increased use of advanced alloys of lithium and aluminium. The gradual acceptance of these high-technology materials

The McDonnell Douglas F/A-18 Hornet is the single most important warplane in the US Navy's carrierborne inventory, for it is a single type that can undertake both the fighter and the attack roles by a simple change of software in the mission computer. The type emerged from the same light-weight fighter technology demonstration programme as the General Dynamics (now Lockheed Martin) F-16 Fighting Falcon, and was originally a Northrop design.

did not indicate any desire for higher performance, but rather the desire to reduce weight without sufficient strength, and to simplify the production and maintenance of complex structures.

In the context of the performance plateau, it is worth noting that experience in combat has provided ample evidence that Mach 2 performance is more than adequate under most operational and tactical conditions; in the Vietnam conflict, the Arab Israeli wars and the Falklands campaign, supersonic combat proved exceptionally rare. Even when combat was initiated at supersonic speed, the combatants were soon slowed to subsonic speed as they lost energy in supersonic manoeuvres. The lesson learnt from these wars therefore, is that while supersonic performance may be useful for the approach to combat and for interception when targets may be engaged beyond visual range, most military aircraft gain little real advantage from supersonic performance. More important are the factors of

good manoeuvrability at high subsonic speed and an armament that includes a gun capable of high rates of fire for short-range engagements where missiles cannot be used.

Manoeuvrability cannot easily be improved on an existing aircraft except in small measure, by palliatives such as special flap settings. However, there are exceptions such as delta-wing aircraft whose agility can be enhanced very considerably by the addition of canard foreplanes. These smooth the airflow over the wing at high angles of attack and, if movable, supplement the trailing edge elevons to produce considerable increases in longitudinal control response. Such foreplanes were added to the IAI Kfir (lion cub), the unlicensed Israeli-built derivative of the Dassault Mirage, to produce the markedly superior Kfir-C2 and its Kfir-C7 upgraded version, and in 1982 the French manufacturer decided to follow IAI's lead and offer a similarly upgraded Mirage III/5 as either new-build aircraft or, as has proved more popular, retrofit of existing aircraft. South Africa later moved along the same path to produce its Atlas Cheetah upgrade of the Mirage III with canard foreplanes, a much revised wing, and more advanced electronics of the same basic type fitted in the Kfir.

During the Vietnam War, the Americans found that their primary Mach 2+ fighters were not proving to be as successful as anticipated against the

When France refused to deliver the Dassault Mirage 5 clear-weather fighters for which it had paid in advance, Israel responded by developing its own derivative of the Mirage III as the IAI Kfir with more advanced Israeli electronics, the more powerful General Electric J79 turbojet and, in its definitive form, canard foreplanes for considerably improved field performance and combat agility.

Now disappearing from service, the Lockheed F-104 Starfighter was developed after the Korean War to provide the US Air Force with a 'manned missile' for the fast-climbing interception role. Only modest numbers were built for the USAF in the interceptor and adapted tactical fighter roles, but then came very large orders for the F-104G multi-role fighter version.

133

The Dassault Mirage 2000 is an extremely capable multi-role warplane that uses modern aerodynamics, a design of relaxed static stability, and a fly-by-wire control system to overcome the energy-sapping tendencies of the delta wing planform in lower-altitude manoeuvring flight.

less advanced Mikoyan-Gurevich fighters operated by the North Vietnamese air force. It was this air campaign that revealed the value of agility at high subsonic speeds, when the MiG-17 'Fresco', MiG-19 'Farmer' and MiG-21 'Fishbed' fighters managed to outfly machines such as the F-100 Super Sabre, Lockheed F-104 Starfighter, F-105 Thunderchief, F-4 Phantom II and F-8 Crusader. The US forces, and especially the US Air Force, instituted a massive research programme that resulted in the creation of two of history's most important military aircraft. The General Dynamics YF-16 prototype proved so superb that it was placed in production as the F-16 Fighting Falcon, while the Northrop YF-17 provided the starting point for the McDonnell Douglas/Northrop F/A-18 Hornet. These aircraft were designed to complement he heavier and less agile McDonnell Douglas F-15 Eagle and Grumman (now Northrop Grumman) F-14 Tomcat respectively, whose origins pre-dated the experiences of Vietnam. While the heavier fighters had a power-to-weight ratio close to or exceeding unity, which gave them excellent speed and rate of climb for the interceptor role, the lighter fighters were machines with less outright performance but far greater agility in the air combat role.

The F-16 was among the first service aircraft (with the Panavia Tornado) to use 'fly-by-wire' control, in which the pilot is linked to his control surfaces not by mechanical or hydraulic systems, but by means of computer-

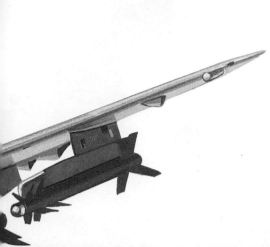

connected electrical impulses. In this system the pilot's control inputs are correlated by the computer with air data and other factors to decide the optimum control responses needed to satisfy the pilot's basic demands. The use of such a system also permits the relaxation of the previously rigid relationship between the centre of gravity and the centre of pressure, resulting in an aeroplane that is inherently unstable, can only be flown via the 'fly-by-wire' system, and is therefore superbly agile.

Major strides have also been made in the aerodynamics of agility, notably in the development of leading-edge root extensions (LERXes) by Northrop for its YF-17 experimental fighter. These LERXes are highly important in the F/A-18 Hornet, and have been incorporated in the Northrop F-5 Tiger II light fighter; they were also featured in the superb Northrop F-20A Tigershark multi-role fighter that could have entered service in the late 1980s or early 1990s but failed to secure a production order for a variety of reasons, many of them politically inspired. Other aerodynamic advances have been made possible by the development of new materials that permit the use of forward-swept wings, which offer the same advantages as the swept-back wing while affording distinct improvement in flight at high angles of attack.

Although it was weel known that the Soviets' huge numerical advantage over the Western alliance was more than counterbalanced by the technical superiority of weapons fielded by the West, it became clear through the 1970s and 1980s that the Soviets were rapidly closing the technological gap. Indeed, this fact was stunningly revealed when the West was first allowed to gain a glimpse of two new-generation Soviet combat aircraft, the Mikoyan-Gurevich MiG-29 'Fulcrum' and Sukhoi Su-27 'Flanker', which appeared in the late 1980s as the Soviet counterparts of the F-16 and F-15. Exhibition flights demonstrated that both Soviet aircraft possessed incredible agility,

The Northrop (now Northrop Grumman) F-5 series was developed in the later 1950s to provide the less technically sophisticated of the USA's allies with a slightly supersonic warplane that could use small and poorly equipped air bases, would be cheap to buy and affordable to operate, and yet would still provide useful capabilities for defensive warfare. The series started with the F-5A single-seat fighter and F-5B two-seat trainer variants of the radarless Freedom Fighter model, and then progressed to the F-5E single-seat fighter and F-5F combat-capable two-seat trainer of the radar-fitted Tiger II series with a number of aerodynamic improvements as well as an uprated powerplant.

Although it was conceived solely for experimental purposes, the Grumman X-29A shows a possible way forward for warplane design. The aeroplane is a canard type of the relaxed static stability subvariant controllable only via a fly-by-wire system and is therefore very agile, while the adoption of forward-swept wings, made resistant to twisting by their special composite construction, offers all the advantages of rearward-swept wings together with several advantages in lower-speed handling.

and the release of further information revealed excellent overall performance, the ability to carry large loads of advanced weapons, and electronic capabilities generally equal to those of their Western counterparts, and in some areas (notably the IR search and track sensors) superior to anything available in the West.

The technologically and industrially advanced nations of the Western alliance are gradually overhauling this marginal Russian lead, however, with a new generation of combat aircraft. The US Air Force, for example, began to operate very small numbers of the Lockheed (now Lockheed Martin) F-117 Sky Knight 'stealthy' attack fighter and Northrop Grumman B-2 Spirit strategic bomber from 1983 and 1994 respectively, and another advanced type scheduled for delivery early in the next century is the Lockheed Martin/Boeing F-22 Rapier advanced tactical fighter. These aircraft mark a quantum advance over their predecessors in terms of low-observability, which is the 'stealthiness' that allows them to operate with minimal chance

The CF-18A is the Canadian land-based counterpart of the McDonnell Douglas F/A-18A Hornet single-seat fighter and attack warplane operated by the US Navy and US Marine Corps, but differs on no significant detail from the F/A-18 baseline version.

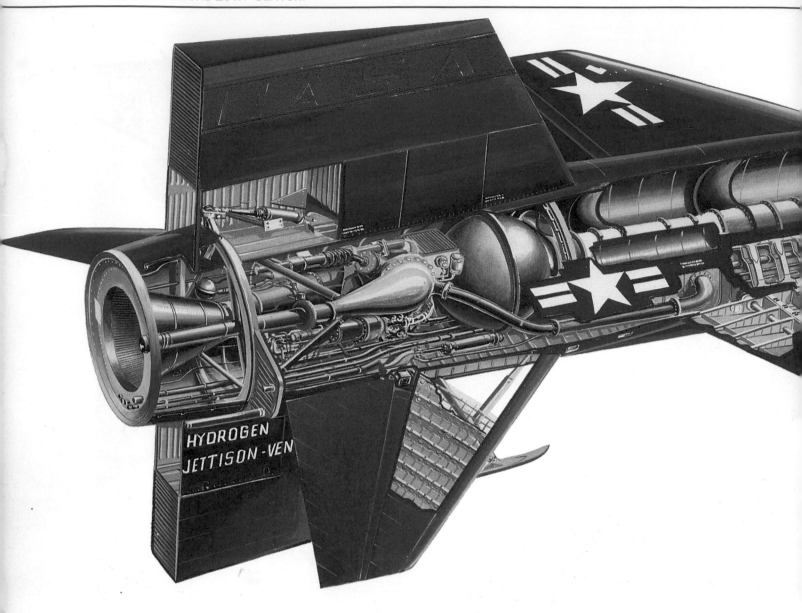

HYDROGEN
JETTISON-VEN

Another type that was conceived and operated exclusively in the experimental arena, the North American X-15 was a rocket-powered type launched at high altitude from a motherplane for the exploration of highly supersonic flight conditions in the upper atmosphere, or rather in the interface between the atmosphere and space, and for the testing of ablative coatings for re-entry vehicles. Even so, many of the lessons learned with the X-15 were applied to later generations of military aircraft.

of detection by any enemy air-defence systems. This 'stealthiness' is derived from very careful internal and external design to minimise angles or flat sections that can reflect radar signals, equally careful design of the exterior surfaces and engine exhausts to minimise visual, acoustic and thermal signatures, and reliance on passive sensors in place of earlier aircraft's active sensors such as radar. (A radar beam is as 'visible' in its sector of the electromagnetic spectrum as the light beam of a lighthouse on a dark night in the visual light sector of the spectrum.) The emphasis on such aircraft, in terms of development urgency and procurement totals, has been scaled down following the collapse of the former USSR, but the fact that US forces may still face high-technology threats in other parts of the world is constantly borne in mind.

Russia is still actively involved in the development of advanced combat aircraft, but is beset by political and financial problems, and is therefore unlikely to emerge as a realistic successor to the USSR in terms of military power. The country inherited the bulk of the USSR's military machine, with lesser portions going to the Ukraine and the other ex-Soviet republics that now constitute the CIS.

It was the threat from the USSR that spurred the development of other

modern weapons for the Western bloc. So far as aircraft are concerned, these range from light multi-role tactical fighters such as the Italo-Brazilian AMX to advanced tactical combat aircraft such as the Dassault Rafale (squall) for the French air force and naval air arm, and the Eurofighter 2000 for the British, German, Italian and Spanish air forces. The AMX is operational, and the Rafale and Eurofighter 2000 are due to enter service at the beginning of the next century, although some of the programmes' most advanced elements have been curtailled and planned procurement has been scaled down. It is worth noting that the Rafale and Eurofighter 2000, together with the JAS 39 Gripen (griffon) that is further advanced towards production for the Swedish air force, are of the 'modern' configuration with canard foreplanes and an aft-mounted delta wing controlled via a 'fly-by-wire' system for extreme agility and the capability to fly at very high angles of attack.

All three Western types are inherently 'stealthy', have advanced powerplants offering a very high power-to-weight ratio in afterburner, and have electronics based on a digital databus system for the maximum exploitation of active and passive sensors, advanced computers, and the very latest in disposable weapons. These are all features of the combat aircraft ofthe next century.

The Lockheed Martin F-117 Night Hawk is a 'stealthy' attack warplane designed for subsonic flight but possessing the ability to tackle and destroy high-value point targets with precision-guided munitions by using its special structure and design to avoid detection and therefore interception and destruction.

Glossary

AFTERBURNING system to inject and burn additional fuel with the unburned oxygen in a turbine engine's exhaust and thereby generate additional thrust; also known as reheat

ANHEDRAL negative angle at which a wing or tailplane section is installed relative to the lateral datum

BIPLANE aeroplane with two sets of flying surfaces one above the other

CANNON rapid-fire weapon firing ammunition with an explosive projectile

DIHEDRAL positive angle at which a wing or tailplane section is installed relative to the lateral datum

GULL type of wing with an angled joint at which the sharply dihedralled inboard section becomes less acutely dihedralled

INLINE type of aero engine with the cylinders arranged in one or more longitudinal rows

INTERRUPTER equipment to synchronise the firing of a machine-gun with the rotation of the propeller and thus prevent a blade being hit by a machine gun bullet

INVERTED GULL type of wing with an angled joint at which the sharply anhedralled inboard section becomes a dihedralled outboard section

LAMINAR FLOW type of wing specially designed to ensure a smooth flow of the boundary-layer air past the surface of the wing and so reduce drag and turbulence

MACHINE-GUN rapid-fire weapon firing ammunition with a 'ball' (solid) projectile

MONOPLANE aeroplane with a single set of flying surfaces

PARASOL type of monoplane in which the wing is carried above the fuselage

PISTON ENGINE type of aero engine that develops its power by the reciprocating movement of pistons in cylinders as a result of the burning of a fuel/air mix in the cylinders, this reciprocating movement in the cylinders being turned into rotary power by the action of connecting rods on the crankshaft

PUSHER with a propeller that pushes the aeroplane forward

RADIAL type of aero engine with the cylinders arranged in one or two radial rows around the crankshaft

REHEAT system to inject and burn additional fuel with the unburned oxygen in a turbine engineís exhaust and thereby generate additional thrust; also known as afterburning

ROTARY type of aero engine similar in arrangement to the radial engine but with the crankshaft bolted to the airframe and remaining stationary as the rest of the engine, with the propeller attached, rotates

SESQUIPLANE biplane with the smaller wing considerably smaller than the upper wing

TRACTOR with a propeller that pulls the aeroplane forward

TRIPLANE aeroplane with three sets of flying surfaces one above the other

TURBOFAN turbine engine combining turbojet and turboprop features in as much as the turbine stage powers a large-diameter forward fan whose central column of air is drawn into the compressor and whose outer cylinder of lower-velocity air passes round the core engine

TURBOJET type of aero engine that develops its power by the use of a system to compress air, which is then mixed with fuel and burned to create a powerful exhaust that drives the turbine system powering the compressor and generating thrust turboprop turbine engine in which the exhaust-powered turbine drives a propeller and produces only a small residual thrust

Index

A

AEG G II 26
AEG G IV 26
Airco (de Havilland) D.H.2 14, 15
Airco (de Havilland) D.H.4 29
Airco (de Havilland) D.H.9/9a 28,
  29
Albatros 8, 12
Albatros B II 8-9
Albatros D I 17
Albatros D II 17
Albatros D III 12
Albatros D III 17
Albatros D V/Va 22
Amiot 143 35
Amiot 350 44
AMX International AMX 138-139
Ansaldo SVA 18, 25
Arado Ar 234 Blitz 72, 74-75, 107
Armstrong Whitworth F.K.8 17, 22
Armstrong Whitworth Siskin 34,
  35
Armstrong Whitworth Whitley 45,
  60-61
Atlas Cheetah 96
Aviatik 8, 10
Avro Anson 70
Avro Lancaster 61, 63
Avro Shackleton 116
Avro Vulcan 111-112

B

BAC TSR-2 102
BAe Harrier 130-131
Bell P-39 Airacobra 76
Bell P-59 Airacomet 85
Blackburn Buccaneer 102-103
Blériot 8
Bloch M.B.151 44
Bloch M.B.175 44
Bloch M.B.200 35, 36
Boeing AGM-86 120
Boeing B-9 35, 38
Boeing B-17 Flying Fortress 45, 63
Boeing B-29 Superfortress 80
Boeing B-47 Stratojet 110
Boeing B-50 108-109
Boeing B-52 Stratofortress 110-111,
  120

Boeing E-3 Sentry 122, 123
Boeing F2B 38
Boeing F4B 32-33, 38
Boeing P-12 38
Boeing P-26 'Peashooter' 38-39
Boeing PW-9 38
Boelcke, Oswald 14
Boulton & Paul Sidestrand 34
Breguet Bre.14 11, 13, 29
Breguet Bre.690 44
Breguet Bre.1050 Alizé 101, 102
Brewster F2A Buffalo 76
Bristol Beaufighter 56, 70
Bristol Bulldog 36
Bristol F.2 Fighter 16, 22, 34
Bristol Scout D 9

C

Caproni Ca 3 28, 29
Caproni Ca 4 28
Caproni Ca 45 30-31
Caproni Ca 5 28
Chengdu F-7M Airguard 103
Chengdu J-7 103
Consolidated B-24 Liberator 63, 65,
  71
Consolidated PBY Catalina 70-71
Convair B-36 109
Convair B-58 Hustler 106, 112
Convair F-102 Delta Dagger 99
Convair F-106 Delta Dart 99
Curtiss Falcon 39
Curtiss Hawk 38
Curtiss P-36 45
Curtiss P-40 Kittyhawk and
  Warhawk 45, 68-70, 76
Curtiss P-6 38
Curtiss SB2C Helldiver 80

D

Dassault Atlantic 1 116
Dassault Atlantique 2 116-117
Dassault Etendard 101
Dassault Mirage 2000 123, 126,
  134
Dassault Mirage 4000 119
Dassault Mirage 5 95-96, 133
Dassault Mirage F1 95, 126
Dassault Mirage III 94-95, 133
Dassault Mystére 93-94
Dassault Ourgan 93
Dassault Rafale 139

Dassault Super Mystére 93-94
Dassault/Dornier Alpha Jet 118
de Havilland D.H.9a 34
de Havilland Hornet 73
de Havilland Mosquito 59-60, 70,
  98
de Havilland Sea Vixen 102
de Havilland Vampire 81, 82-83, 84,
  85
Dewoitine D.500 37, 38
Dewoitine D.520 44
DFW C IV 25
DFW C V 25
Dornier Do 17 41, 49
Douglas AD/A-1 Skyraider 101
Douglas A3D/A-3 Skywarrior 101
Douglas A4D/A-4 Skyhawk 101
Douglas DB-7 45
Douglas F3D Skyknight 101
Douglas SBD Dauntless 46-47, 72,
  80

E

English Electric Canberra 116
English Electric Lightning 94
Etrich Taube 8
Eurofighter 2000 139

F

Fairchild Republic A-10
  Thunderbolt II 126, 128, 130-131
Fairey Albacore 55
Fairey Barracuda 102
Fairey Fawn 34
Fairey Firefly 102
Fairey Flycatcher 40, 44
Fairey Fox 36
Fairey Gannet 102
Farman F.60 Goliath 31
Farman F.221 35
Fiat CR.32 39, 43
Fiat CR.42 39, 43
Fiat G.50 Freccia 43
Fiat G91 99
Fieseler Fi 156 Storch 48
Focke-Wulf Fw 190 56, 73
Focke-Wulf Fw 200 Condor 70-72
Focke-Wulf Ta 152 73
Fokker D VII 22-24
Fokker D VIII 22
Fokker Dr I 19, 20-21
Fokker Dr I 22

Fokker E I 13
Fokker E II 14
Fokker E III 14
Fokker E series 15
Fokker Eindecker 17
Fokker M 5 Eindecker 13
Fokker, Anthony 13
Friedrichshafen G II 26
Friedrichshafen G III 26

G

Garros, Roland 12
General Dynamics F-111 112-113
General Dynamics F-16 Fighting
    Falcon 119, 134
Gloster Gauntlet 36, 41
Gloster Gladiator 36, 44-45, 52
Gloster Grebe 34, 35
Gloster Javelin 108
Gloster Meteor 73, 85
Gotha G III 26
Gotha G IV 27
Gotha G V 27
Grumman F4F Wildcat 76-77
Grumman F6F Hellcat 80
Grumman F8F Bearcat 101
Grumman F9F Panther and Cougar
    101
Grumman TBF Avenger 76-77, 80,
    102
Grumman X-29 136

H

Halberstadt C V 25
Halberstadt CL II 24, 30
Handley Page Halifax 61, 71
Handley Page Hampden 45, 60, 61
Handley Page Heyford 34, 35
Handley Page O/100 29
Handley Page O/400 28-29
Handley Page V/1500 29
Handley Page Victor 111-112
Hannover CL II 18, 30
Hannover CL III 30
Hawker Fury 36, 58-59, 73
Hawker Hart 36
Hawker Hind 36
Hawker Hunter 93
Hawker Hurricane 44-45, 58, 69
Hawker Sea Fury 102
Hawker Sea Hawk 102
Hawker Typhoon 54, 66

Hawker Siddeley Harrier 119
Hawker Siddeley Nimrod 116
Heinkel He 111 41, 49, 52-53, 72
Heinkel He 178 45
Heinkel He 51 41, 42
Henschel Hs 123 49

I

IAI Kfir 96, 119, 133
IAI Nesher and Dagger 96
Ilyushin A-50 122, 123
Ilyushin Il-2 59
Ilyushin Il-4 59
Ilyushin Il-28 98, 116
Ilyushin Il-38 117
Ilyushin Il-76 122

J

Junkers J 1 29
Junkers Ju 52/3m 41
Junkers Ju 87 41, 49, 50-51, 54
Junkers Ju 88 41, 49, 62, 72, 73, 98
Junkers Ju 287 107

L

Lioré-et-Olivier LeO 451 44
Lockheed F-94 Starfire 89
Lockheed F-104 Starfighter 89, 133
Lockheed Hudson 70
Lockheed Martin F-16 Fighting
    Falcon 120-121, 126, 130
Lockheed Martin F-117 Sky Knight
    136-137, 139
Lockheed Martin SR-71 122
Lockheed Martin TR-1 122
Lockheed Martin/Boeing F-22
    Rapier 137
Lockheed P-3 Orion 116
Lockheed P-38 Lightning 64
Lockheed P-80 Shooting Star 85-
    86, 88
Lockheed P2V/P-2 Neptune 84-85,
    116
Lockheed S-3 Viking 103, 122
Lockheed U-2 122
Lockheed YF-12 122
Loire/Gourdou-Leseurre 32 37
LTV A-7 Corsair II 101
LVG 11
LVG C V 25
LVG C VI 25

M

Macchi MB-326 99
Macchi MC.200 Satta 43
Martin B-10 35, 38
Martin B-26 Marauder 66, 78-79
Martin Maryland 45
McDonnell Douglas A-4 Skyhawk
    96-97
McDonnell Douglas F-4 Phantom II
    99-100
McDonnell Douglas F-15 Eagle
    125, 126, 128-129
McDonnell Douglas F/A-18 Hornet
    119, 126, 132, 137
McDonnell Douglas/BAe AV-8
    Harrier II 117, 131-132
McDonnell F-101 Voodoo 96
McDonnell F2H Banshee 101
McDonnell F3H Demon 101
Messerschmitt Bf 109 41, 48-49, 54
Messerschmitt Bf 110 48-49, 54, 62
Messerschmitt Me 163 Komet 73
Messerschmitt Me 262 72, 75, 85
Mikoyan-Gurevich MiG-1 59
Mikoyan-Gurevich MiG-15 86-87
Mikoyan-Gurevich MiG-17 89-90,
    134
Mikoyan-Gurevich MiG-19 90-91,
    134
Mikoyan-Gurevich MiG-21 103-104,
    134
Mikoyan-Gurevich MiG-23 124,
    126
Mikoyan-Gurevich MiG-27 126
Mikoyan-Gurevich MiG-29 136
Mitsubishi A5M 44
Mitsubishi A5M 78
Mitsubishi A6M Reisen 'Zero' 76
Mitsubishi G3M 44
Mitsubishi G4M 44
Morane-Saulnier 8, 11
Morane-Saulnier M.S.406 44
Morane-Saulnier Type L 12
Myasishchyev M-4 114
Myasischchyev M-17/55 122

N

Nakajima Ki-27 44
Nieuport Type 11 Bébé 14, 15
Nieuport Type 17 15
Nieuport-Delage NiD.62 37
North American B-25 Mitchell 66

North American F-86 Sabre 86-87
North American F-100 Super Sabre 88, 134
North American P-51 Mustang 64, 66, 67, 84
North American P-82 Twin Mustang 73, 79
North American X-15 138-139
Northrop F-20 Tigershark 135
Northrop YF-17 134
Northrop Grumman B-2 Spirit 137
Northrop Grumman E-2 Hawkeye 124
Northrop Grumman EA-6 Prowler 125
Northrop Grumman EF-111 Raven 125
Northrop Grumman F-14 Tomcat 126-127
Northrop Grumman F-5 Freedom Fighter and Tiger II 134-135

P

Panavia Tornado 117, 118-119, 125, 126, 134
Petlyakov Pe-2 59
Polikarpov I-15 41
Polikarpov I-15bis 41
Polikarpov I-153 39, 41
Polikarpov I-16 41
Potez Type 63 44
PZL P.7 39
PZL P.11 39, 50-52
PZL P.23 Karas 52
PZL P.24 39
PZL P.37 Los 52, 53

R

Reggiane Re.2000 Sagittario 43
Republic F-84 Thunderjet, Thunderstreak and Thunderflash 86, 91
Republic F-105 Thunderchief 91-93, 134
Republic P-47 Thunderbolt 64, 73, 75
Rockwell B-1 Lancer 111, 115, 120-122
Royal Aircraft Factory B.E.2 8,9, 11, 20, 25
Royal Aircraft Factory R.E.8 13, 17, 22, 25
Royal Aircraft Factory S.E.5/5a 19, 20, 27
Rumpler C III 26
Rumpler C IV 25
Rumpler C VII 25

S

Saab 35 Draken 115, 117
Saab 37 Viggen 116, 117
Saab 39 Gripen 119, 139
Salmson 2 25
Savoia-Marchetti S.M.79 43
SEPECAT Jaguar 118, 128, 130
ShinMaywa PS-1 117
Short Stirling 61
Short Sunderland 70
Sikorsky Bolshoi 25, 26
Sikorsky Ruskii Vitiaz 26
Sopwith 1!/2-Strutter 15, 16
Sopwith Camel 21-23
Sopwith Pup 15, 16
Sopwith Snipe 34
Sopwith Tabloid 9
Sopwith Triplane 19
SPAD S.7 15, 20
SPAD S.13 6-7, 20
Sukhoi Su-7 104-105
Sukhoi Su-9 105
Sukhoi Su-11 105
Sukhoi Su-15 105-106
Sukhoi Su-17 105
Sukhoi Su-24 126
Sukhoi Su-25 126, 130
Sukhoi Su-27 136
Supermarine Attacker 102
Supermarine Scimitar 102
Supermarine Seafire 101-102
Supermarine Spiteful 73
Supermarine Spitfire 44-45, 56-57, 66
Supermarine Swift 93

T

Tupolev ANT-5 (I-4) 43
Tupolev ANT-6 41
Tupolev Tu-4 108
Tupolev Tu-16 113
Tupolev Tu-22 114-115, 120
Tupolev Tu-22M 115, 120
Tupolev Tu-28 106
Tupolev Tu-95 100, 114
Tupolev Tu-126 123
Tupolev Tu-160 120

U

Ufag C I 25

V

V-1 73
V-2 107
Vickers F.B.5 'Gunbus' 15
Vickers Valiant 110-111
Vickers Vimy 34
Vickers Virginia 34
Vickers Wellington 45, 60-61, 62
Voisin 8, 10
Vought F4U Corsair 80, 101
Vought Crusader 101, 134

W

Wels Taube 8
Wibault 72 37
Witteman-Lewis NBL-1 34

Y

Yakovlev Yak-28 84-85, 105
Yakovlev Yak-38 132
Yakovlev Yak-141 132

Z

Zeppelin (Staaken) R VI 27
Zeppelin airships 10, 26-27